Praise for *Survi...*

"In *Surviving Parental Alienation*, A... ...ul and tragic stories of parental alienation and, in doing so, honor the parents and children who have suffered because of parental alienation. They provide a deeper understanding of why people find and marry people who will eventually alienate their children from them, how the alienating parents 'sell' the poisonous message to the children, and how—sometimes when it seems least likely—the alienated children and their lost parents find their way back to each other. This is a moving book and a must-read for parents and professionals alike." —**S. Richard Sauber**, PhD, ABPP, family forensic psychologist and editor of the *American Journal of Family Therapy*

"An important and powerful book—for parents and professionals! Baker and Fine have combined tragic stories of children rejecting a parent with a solid analysis of the often-hidden behaviors that lead to such alienation. But most of all, they have included stories of hope and reconciliation (equally including fathers and mothers who have been *targets of blame*), with effective strategies for parents who want to reach out to their alienated children. This book helps show the importance of understanding alienating behaviors and, without focusing on blame, but rather what to do now with many excellent suggestions." —**Bill Eddy**, family lawyer, family therapist, and coauthor of *Splitting: Protecting Yourself While Divorcing Someone with Borderline Personality Disorder*

"*Surviving Parental Alienation* is a work that will help reduce the emotional isolation that an alienated parent feels. The authors give the alienated parent hope and reason for not giving up and walking away from the children they love dearly." —**Douglas Darnall**, PhD, author of *Beyond Divorce Casualties: Reunifying the Alienated Family*

Surviving Parental Alienation

A Journey of Hope and Healing

Amy J. L. Baker and Paul R. Fine

ROWMAN & LITTLEFIELD
Lanham • Boulder • New York • Toronto • Plymouth, UK

Published by Rowman & Littlefield
4501 Forbes Boulevard, Suite 200, Lanham, Maryland 20706
www.rowman.com

10 Thornbury Road, Plymouth PL6 7PP, United Kingdom

British Library Cataloguing in Publication Information Available

Library of Congress Cataloging-in-Publication Data

Baker, Amy J. L.
Surviving parental alienation : a journey of hope and healing / Amy J. L. Baker and Paul R. Fine.
pages cm
Includes bibliographical references and index.
ISBN 978-1-4422-2677-7 (cloth : alk. paper) — ISBN 978-1-4422-2678-4 (electronic)
1. Parent and child. 2. Parent and adult child. 3. Parental alienation syndrome. 4. Alienation (Social psychology) 5. Children of divorced parents—Counseling of. I. Fine, Paul R., 1955– II. Title.
HQ755.85.B3347 2014
302.5'44—dc23
2013045191

♾™ The paper used in this publication meets the minimum requirements of American National Standard for Information Sciences Permanence of Paper for Printed Library Materials, ANSI/NISO Z39.48-1992.

Printed in the United States of America

We dedicate this book to our parents and our children,
from whom we have learned so much about forgiveness, hope, and
healing, and to parents and children affected by alienation. May they all
come home to each other.

Contents

Acknowledgments

We would like to gratefully acknowledge the wonderful team at Rowman & Littlefield, including Kathryn Knigge, who shepherded the book through the process and was helpful at every turn. The book has been greatly improved through the careful and attentive editorial skills of Naomi Mindlin. We extend a special acknowledgment to our darling daughter Alianna, who assisted in many ways throughout this project. We also would like to thank the many parents who wrote (and tried to write) their stories for the book. They are unsung heroes.

Chapter One

Introduction

And this is why
We tell the story.
Why we tell the story . . .
Life is why . . . ,
Pain is why . . . ,
Love is why . . . ,
Grief is why . . . ,
Hope is why . . . ,
Faith is why . . . ,
You are why. . . .
So I hope that you will tell this tale tomorrow.
It will help your heart remember and relive.
It will help you feel the anger and the sorrow
And forgive. . . .
For out of what we live and we believe
Our lives become
The stories that we weave.
　　　—Lynn Ahrens from *Once on This Island*[1]

It is a fairly routine occurrence for a professional in the field of parental alienation to receive an e-mail from a targeted parent asking if she would like to hear that parent's parental alienation story (sometimes the person simply sends the story without asking) or asks her if she would like to write a book about that parent's experience with parental alienation. Many of these parents explain that someone (usually an attorney or custody evaluator) has informed them that they have the worst case of parental alienation ever seen, and these parents have become convinced that something good can come

1

from their telling their story. They are deeply invested in sharing their ordeal with others in the hope that they and others can gain something by doing so.

WHY WE TELL AND READ STORIES OF PAIN AND HARDSHIP

The reasons why targeted parents want to tell their story are varied and all of them are valid and easily understandable. Some desire an emotional release through the retelling of the story or want to warn others of pitfalls and mistakes to avoid. For other parents, the impetus is to try to rise above their pain by turning it into a narrative, an external object that resides outside of them. In this way they separate and detach from the emotional pull of their parental alienation trauma. Some parents seek validation and understanding for their parental alienation journey, which too often involves feeling blamed, shamed, and misunderstood by friends, family, and professionals. Yet another reason to write their story is to process it in a new and deeper way, to come to a new understanding of what has transpired. They hope that perhaps, finally, they can arrive at a resolution or solution, or just find some meaning where before they could not find any.

They are right to want to share their story. They *do* have something of value to share. Their story *is* important. Each story has something to teach, something universal about the human spirit and about a parent's love for his/her child, as well as something specific about parental alienation.

Yet another reason to share one's story is to offer a vision of hope and healing for those who have not yet achieved their desired outcome. Unfortunately, stories of successful reunifications of formerly alienated children are relatively rare in the literature. This may be because of survivor's guilt at having succeeded where others have—to date—failed, or it may be because newly reconciled parents have no time to write their story, as they are preoccupied with the formidable task of reengaging with their lost child. There may also be a desire to forget the whole ordeal rather than relive the agonizing details of one's pain, loss, and suffering.

This has been unfortunate because reading stories can be as helpful as writing stories. Mental health professionals have identified several potential benefits from reading other people's accounts of challenges and difficulties—for example, those benefits discussed in "Organizing for Bibliotherapy: The Science of the Art."[2] In "The Power of Stories/Stories about Power," Baker identifies the ways in which reading stories about parental alienation can be healing, including the following.[3]

Engagement

Currently targeted parents who are in the midst of a custody conflict and/or parental alienation drama may appreciate the stories of other's alienation because no matter how empathetic a therapist is, a targeted parent may still feel alone in the situation until reading someone else's similar story. The specificity offered by a narrative account is unparalleled as a means of providing an opportunity for the identification and satisfaction of the need for a shared experience. Thus, targeted parents can gain a sense of engagement with the social world through the process of reading others' stories. In *The Healing Power of Stories,* psychologist Daniel Taylor writes, "We tell and listen to stories to reassure ourselves that we are not home alone. Our fear of isolation is instinctive and profound. Every story is evidence that someone else is out there."[4]

Empowerment

Reading other parents' true accounts of parental alienation experiences can also help alleviate a targeted parent's feelings of rage and helplessness that justifiably accompany being the victim of an injustice such as parental alienation. Knowing that others have experienced the same level of frustration and despair may counter the belief that one has been personally singled out for such suffering. If the stories are able to portray the targeted parent—while imperfect, as all humans are—as unmistakably a victim of the other parent's malicious and devious plan to turn the children against them, undeserving of their child's hatred and rejection, then the stories can serve as an antidote to the blame and shame targeted parents may feel. Stories can clarify that the targeted parent did not deserve the alienation and that a larger systemic problem (the adversarial legal system, a personality disorder of the alienating parent, vulnerabilities within the child) exacerbated the alienation drama. This realization can also be empowering.

Education/Enhancement

Reading stories of other parents' alienation ordeals can provide the reader with an opportunity to explore alternative attitudes and choices, and if the opportunity allows for it, the reader may ask him-/herself, "Would I make that choice? What do I think would happen if I had acted as that parent had?" Because narratives allow for identification with the characters in the story, the reader can "try on" a range of attitudes and interactional styles and imagine what they would feel like. This could result in a new way of thinking, acting, and feeling. Readers may identify specific strategies and techniques for dealing with parental alienation that they had not considered before. Or perhaps reading stories of other parents' alienation ordeals can result in greater confidence in one's choices.

Encouragement

Readers can find inspiration and encouragement from the stories because many involve targeted parents persevering against tremendous odds. Through these stories, the reader is bearing witness to the heroic strength and dedication targeted parents have to their children, and thus symbolically bears witness to his/her own strength and dedication. This process can motivate and encourage the reader to forge on despite the obstacles and hurdles that previously seemed overwhelming. Reading stories in which the targeted parent did not prevail (as painful a prospect as that is) can show that it is possible to have a meaningful life despite the loss and sadness. As educator and national storyteller Diane Rooks notes in *Spinning Gold Out of Straw: How Stories Heal*, "As we share stories of endurance and resilience with others, we reinforce the possibility that they too can survive."[5]

Enlightenment

Reading stories of other targeted parents' journeys reinforces the idea that we are all imperfect humans doing the best we can in a very imperfect world. Readers can see that targeted parents make mistakes along the way. They choose future mates who are selfish, immature, controlling, and unable to value them as spouses and parents of their children. Targeted parents also make mistakes in how they respond to the unfolding alienation drama. They don't have the benefit of hindsight to know exactly what the right move will be in each situation. The reader can identify with the story's protagonist, and thereby gain a clearer understanding of his/her own role in his/her own parental alienation journey. Every targeted parent can learn from the missteps of others. At the same time, being empathetic with the protagonist—despite his/her foibles—may allow the reader to metaphorically forgive and practice greater compassion to him-/herself.

For all of these reasons, we decided to pull together some of the best stories we could find on parental alienation and to include some about successful reunifications. To do that, we reached out to parents who have contacted us over the years to invite them to write their stories. Some stories are included in full in this book, while others are alluded to throughout the book in order to illustrate a particular point. We invite you, the reader, to share your stories with us so that we can join together to become better educated and more empowered, enlightened, inspired, and motivated to work harder to stop this unnecessary and still generally unacknowledged, but extremely painful, form of emotional abuse of children.

PARENTAL ALIENATION 101

To set the stage for the stories and discussion to come, we begin with a brief overview of parental alienation. *Parental alienation* is the term used to describe a family dynamic in which one parent (referred to as the *alienating* or *favored parent*) engages in behaviors (referred to as *alienation strategies*) to foster a child's unjustified rejection of and disaffection for the other parent (referred to as the *rejected* or *targeted parent*). Not all children exposed to these behaviors succumb to the pressure to reject the other parent, but when they do, they exhibit telltale signs (referred to as the *behavioral manifestations of parental alienation*) and they can be considered as having the parental alienation syndrome, or being an alienated child.

There are a few points of controversy within the field, such as whether this phenomenon can properly be called a *syndrome*, whether the alienating parents are acting intentionally, when and which treatments are recommended, and to what extent the rejected parent contributes to the problem, but there is no disagreement that the dynamic exists and that it is harmful to children. Our positions on these points of disagreements are as follows:

1. We believe that it should be considered a syndrome that manifests within the child, as it meets the American Psychiatric Association's definition of a *syndrome* in the fifth edition of the *Diagnostic and Statistical Manual of Mental Disorders*: "A grouping of signs and symptoms, based on their frequent co-occurrence that may suggest a common underlying pathogenesis, course, familial pattern, or treatment selection."[6]
2. We contend that it generally does not matter whether the alienating parent is consciously and intentionally engaging in these behaviors,

and that most likely some are conscious and intentional, while others are not.

3. We believe that there are effective treatments currently in operation that are available to families when judges act decisively to enable families to participate.

4. We also have observed that all parents are imperfect and, therefore, many custody evaluators and judges who prefer to believe that both parents are at fault will always have some action of the targeted parent to point to in order to bolster that belief. Often those flaws are not causative of the alienation and are in fact greatly outweighed by the flaws of the favored parent.

5. We wholeheartedly reject the notion that Janet Johnston promotes in "Parental Alignments and Rejection: An Empirical Study of Alienation in Children of Divorce" that targeted parents "are the architects of their own rejection."[7] In fact, we have observed that the "hybrid model" proclaiming that all parties play a hand in the alienation is used as a crutch for evaluators and judges who do not want to make bold decisions. They prefer to spread the blame around as an excuse to not take action.

Despite these areas of disagreement, substantial consensus exists. A growing body of empirical research now supports the major tenets of parental alienation theory. Specifically, research has consistently identified a set of parental behaviors that foster a child's unjustified rejection of the targeted parent. These parents have been identified by adults who experienced alienation as children, as Baker reports in *Adult Children of Parental Alienation Syndrome: Breaking the Ties that Bind*,[8] as well as by targeted parents themselves, as Baker and Darnall report in "Behaviors and Strategies of Parental Alienation: A Survey of Parental Experiences."[9]

Subsequent research has demonstrated the validity of these behaviors. For example, in several studies, Baker and colleagues report associations between the strategies and psychological maltreatment or measures of well-being: "Adult Recall of Parental Alienation in a Community Sample: Prevalence and Associations with Psychological Maltreatment," "Adolescents Caught in Their Parents' Loyalty Conflicts," "College Student Childhood Exposure to Parental Loyalty Conflicts," "Italian College Student Childhood Exposure to Parental Loyalty Conflicts," and "To Turn a Child Against a Parent Is to Turn a Child Against Himself."[10] Across all of the studies, the greater the number of behaviors endorsed, the lower the self-esteem, the greater the likelihood of endorsement of an insecure style of attachment, and the greater the likelihood of endorsement of psychological symptoms.

The seventeen behaviors identified as parental alienation strategies are presented in table 1.1, along with examples and a brief explanation as to how they work.

Taken together, these seventeen parental alienation strategies create psychological distance between the child and the targeted parent such that the relationship becomes conflict ridden and eventually nonexistent, as the child is empowered (if not pressured) to cut that parent off completely. Each of these behaviors serve to

1. further the child's cohesion and alignment with the alienating parent;
2. create psychological distance between the child and the targeted parent;
3. intensify the targeted parent's anger and hurt over the child's behavior; and
4. incite conflict between the child and the targeted parent.

When exposed to these behaviors, some children eventually and unjustifiably reject the targeted parent altogether, and when that happens the child is said to be *alienated*. There are eight behaviors consistent with unjustified rejection. The labels for these behaviors were first created by noted child psychiatrist Dr. Richard Gardner[11] and have since been validated by Amy Baker and Doug Darnall in "A Construct Study of the Eight Symptoms of Severe Parental Alienation Syndrome: A Survey of Parental Experiences,"[12] as well as by Baker, Burkhard, and Kelly in "Differentiating Alienated From Not Alienated Children: A Pilot Study."[13] Even those who disagree with some of the tenets of parental alienation theory—for example, Joan Kelly and Janet Johnston[14]—concur that these behaviors are clinically significant indicators of alienation. These eight behaviors are presented in table 1.2.

These behaviors are distinctive and highly unusual for children to display in the absence of a strong external impetus. Even horribly abused children who have been beaten and molested by their parents do not exhibit these behaviors.[15] They are typically seen only in children who have been exposed to parental alienation behaviors by one parent in order to foster a child's unjustified rejection of the other parent. When these behaviors are present, the parent-child relationship is seriously ruptured—often for months, if not

Table 1.1.   Parental Alienation Strategies

Parental Alienation Strategy	Examples	Explanation
Badmouthing/ Denigrating the Other Parent	The alienating parent • speaks ill of the other parent to the children and within the children's hearing in a steady stream of negative messaging that is not balanced by anything positive • emphasizes the negative aspects of the other parent's personality and choices • vilifies the other parent in the children's community	Creates the belief in the children that the other parent is unsafe, unloving, and unavailable
Limiting Contact	The alienating parent • interferes with the amount of face-to-face time the children spend with the other parent such as coming early for pick-ups and late for drop-offs • does not produce the children for the other parent's parenting time • shows up during the other parent's parenting time and monopolizes the children's attention	Reduces the targeted parent's opportunities to show him-/herself to be safe, loving, and available, and limits that parent's opportunities to create loving memories and counter the badmouthing message
Interfering with Communication	The alienating parent • makes it difficult for the children and targeted parent to speak on the phone (or communicate by other means) during periods of separation • blocks e-mails and text messages • does not share cell phone numbers • does not answer calls • does not deliver gifts and letters	Prevents the children and targeted parent from sharing in each other's daily lives in a meaningful way

Interfering with Symbolic Communication	The alienating parent • makes it difficult for the children to think about, talk about, or look at pictures of the other parent during periods of separation • eliminates photographs • does not discuss the other parent (unless badmouthing) • discourages the children from thinking about the targeted parent	• Attenuates the children's attachment relationship and feelings of closeness with the targeted parent • Acclimates the children to greater psychological distance • Decreases the importance of the targeted parent in the emotional life of the children
Withholding Love and Approval from the Children	In order to keep their attention directed toward themselves, the alienating parent becomes emotionally cold and distant when the children show positive feelings and thoughts toward the targeted parent	Creates anxiety in the children about losing the love and affection of the alienating parent and heightens the children's need for that parent's approval
Telling the Children That the Targeted Parent Does Not Love Them	The alienating parent • encourages the children to falsely believe that the targeted parent has done things that are hurtful and selfish because that parent does not really care about or value them • conflates the end of the marriage with the end of the targeted parent's love of the children	Creates a feeling in the children of being rejected by the targeted parent, which fosters hurt and anger toward that parent
Allowing/Forcing the Children to Choose Between Parents	By offering desirable alternatives to visitation and/or psychologically pressuring the children to forgo parenting time with the targeted parent, the alienating parent creates situations in which the children will feel compelled to reject the targeted parent	Creates a need in the children to justify their choice, which focuses them on the negative qualities in the targeted parent and incites conflict between the children and the targeted parent, who becomes hurt and angry at the children's choice

Creating the Impression That the Other Parent is Dangerous	The alienating parent does and says things, such as planting false memories of harm or misinterpreting events to falsely create this impression, that suggest or imply that the other parent has or will cause harm to the children	Creates fear and doubt in the minds of the children about the ability of the targeted parent to love them and keep them safe, and also induces hurt and anger in the children
Confiding in the Children	The alienating parent shares personal information with the children about the targeted parent that induces the children to feel anger or shame about that parent and protective of the parent who is engaging in this behavior	Creates psychological distance between the children and the targeted parent, as well as anger and hurt toward the targeted parent based on the misinformation given to them by the alienating parent
Forcing the Children to Reject the Targeted Parent	The alienating parent creates situations in which the children will personally inform the targeted parent that he or she has been excluded from important events in their lives	Incites hurt and anger in the targeted parent and pressure in the children to focus on the negative qualities in the targeted parent in order to justify their rejection of that parent
Asking the Children to Spy on the Targeted Parent	By such requests as asking the children to look through the targeted parent's mail, cell phone call log, or desk drawer, the alienating parent encourages or induces the children to betray the targeted parent's trust	Causes the children to feel angry with the targeted parent for withholding information, a sense of guilt that is then turned into a desire to avoid the parent whom they betrayed, and a need to justify the betrayal by focusing on the negative qualities of that parent
Asking the Children to Keep Secrets from the Targeted Parent	By involving the children's self-interest (e.g., don't tell your father we are going to take a vacation next week because he will try to stop us), the alienating parent encourages the children to withhold important information from the targeted parent despite that parent's having a right or need to have access to that information	Creates a sense of guilt that is then turned into a desire to avoid the parent whom they betrayed, and a need to justify the betrayal by focusing on the negative qualities of that parent

Referring to the Targeted Parent by First Name When Speaking to the Children and/or Encouraging the Children to Do the Same	For example, "Frank is on the phone" or "You just need to tell Jane that you are not going there this weekend."	Conveys to the children that the targeted parent is not an authority figure and is no more important than anyone else whom the children refer to by first name
Referring to a Stepparent as "Mom/Dad" and Encouraging the Children to Do the Same	"This is your new daddy," or "Mommy and I . . ." (when the father is speaking of himself and his new wife)	Replaces the targeted parent with a stepparent and conveys to the children that the alienating parent's new family is the only real and important family to them; this also creates the impression in the children's community (teachers, coaches, and the like) that the replacement parent is the real parent, and creates hurt and anger in the targeted parent
Withholding Medical, Social, Academic Information from the Targeted Parent and Keeping That Parent's Contact Information Off Relevant Forms	The alienating parent does not share team lists, class lists, rosters, schedules, homework assignments, and the like with the targeted parent and does not put that parent's name and number on enrollment and contact forms	Deprives the targeted parent of opportunities to function as a parent and creates the impression that he or she does not care enough to attend important events in the children's lives
Changing the Children's Names to Remove the Association with the Targeted Parent	The alienating parent (if the mother) uses her maiden name or her new spouse/boyfriend's last name as the children's last name, or (if the father) creates a new nickname or uses only his portion of the hyphenated last name	Creates the impression that the targeted parent is not connected to the children in an important and meaningful way
Undermining Authority of the Targeted Parent/Inducing Dependency on Him-/Herself	The alienating parent does and says things that encourage the children to believe that he or she is the only authority figure and that the rules, regulations, and values of the targeted parent are not valid or important	Focuses the children's attention and energy on pleasing the alienating parent and reduces the importance of the targeted parent in the eyes of the children; incites conflict between the children and the targeted parent

Table 1.2.   Child's Behavioral Manifestations of Parental Alienation

Behavior	Example
Campaign of Denigration	The child behaves in a rude, arrogant, disrespectful, and entitled manner toward the targeted parent. The child has no qualms about denigrating that parent to others in the community. The child has difficulty recalling or acknowledging any positive memories of the targeted parent.
Weak, Frivolous, or Absurd Reasons for Rejecting the Targeted Parent	The child will offer reasons such as the floors being scratched or not liking the hairstyle or clothes of the targeted parent. The child will sometimes refuse to even offer a reason, claiming to have done so too many times before when that is not the case.
Lack of Ambivalence toward His/Her Parents	The child claims to worship the alienating parent beyond what is appropriate, necessary, or realistic, while claiming to despise the targeted parent. Both responses are unrealistic and show an inability to see each parent as a mix of good and bad qualities.
Independent Thinker Phenomenon	The child strenuously insists that the alienating parent played no role in his/her rejection of the targeted parent despite the alienating parent's obvious influence.
Lack of Guilt Regarding Poor Treatment of the Targeted Parent	While behaving in a rude and callous manner, the child fails to manifest awareness of or caring about the pain being inflicted on the targeted parent.
Reflexive Support for the Alienating Parent in All Parental Conflicts	The child sides with the alienating parent, no matter how absurd, illogical, or inconsistent that parent's position is.
Presence of Borrowed Scenarios	The child uses words, phrases, and concepts that are not understood, cannot be defined, and are readily attributable to the ideas and beliefs of the alienating parent.
Spread of Animosity to Friends and Family of the Targeted Parent	The child cuts off and/or denigrates formerly beloved friends, neighbors, and family based on their association with the targeted parent.

years. The breach in the relationship is a source of significant pain and suffering for the targeted parent as well as the child. In-depth exploration of the experience from the perspective of adults who were alienated as children clearly demonstrates the devastating short- and long-term negative consequences for the child's well-being, feelings about him-/herself, and ability to function in the world and forge healthy adult relationships (as detailed in Baker's *Adult Children of Parental Alienation Syndrome*). What has been missing from the literature is an equally in-depth exploration of the experience from the perspective of the parents left behind, the parents who spend their days searching for ways to effectively reconnect with their lost children and their nights searching for relief from never-ending pain and loss.

This book was written to take a closer look at the experience of alienation from the point of view of the targeted parent in order to honor their experience and to identify lessons learned from their journeys. Hopefully the reader can learn from both the mistakes and the fruitful actions of those who have gone before, draw strength from their courage, and find hope in their successes.

OVERVIEW OF THE BOOK

In chapter 2 we present four stories about how the future targeted parents met their spouses, fell in love, and had children with their future alienators despite the obvious and not-so-obvious warning signs that the other person was not going to be able to share the children or behave in an honest manner. These stories were solicited from targeted parents and written by them (with editorial input from us). Pseudonyms are used throughout. Chapter 3 highlights the common elements within the stories, focusing on the way in which the future alienators functioned as "wolves in sheep's clothing," masking their desire to exercise power and control over the future targeted parents. Generally, we see these relationships as a perfect storm of a naïve and inexperienced future targeted parent becoming involved with a manipulative and deceitful future alienator. The future targeted parent then proceeds to ignore the obvious red flags, only to become enmeshed in an untenable marriage and disastrous divorce.

In chapter 4 we present three unfolding alienation dramas, explicating how the alienating parent was able to slowly corrupt the child's view and experience of the targeted parent, leading to a complete and total severing of the relationship with the targeted parent. In chapter 5 we explore the stories from the perspective of the tipping point from moderate alienation to severe alienation. Specifically, we examine aspects of the message (that the targeted parent doesn't love the child), aspects of the messenger (the alienating parent's use of known persuasion techniques to sell his/her message to the child), and aspects of the context within which the child and the message reside (the vilification of the targeted parent in the child's community and the selling of alienation to the legal and mental health professionals).

Chapter 6 presents four stories of reconciliation between an alienated child and targeted parent, and chapter 7 highlights relevant themes that can be gleaned from these stories. Specifically, we focus on the catalysts to reconciliation and the numerous things that the targeted parent did right.

In the final two chapters of the book we try to put it all together and explore the common feelings that targeted parents experience while alienated and during the reconciliation process, and we suggest some ways to deal with those feelings. In addition, we offer advice for living and coping with being a targeted parent. We also offer step-by-step suggestions for reaching out to currently alienated adult children.

Throughout the book we pay deep attention to the stories that the targeted parents share with us, to honor those stories and to learn from them. As Freeman observed in *Hindsight*, "[Mindfulness and memory] are both about pausing to attend, whether to past or present; they are about moving from unconsciousness to consciousness; and, not least, they are about living better, more expansively, and with greater awareness of what is real and true."[16]

We invite you to know the struggles and triumphs of others, to join us on this parental alienation odyssey, so that, as in the lyrics of *Once on This Island*, "our lives become the stories that we weave."

Part I

In the Beginning

Chapter Two

Before the Alienation

MARTY'S STORY

How do you know when you found "the one," or, more importantly, did not find her? I wish I had known the answer to that sixteen years ago when I met my ex-wife at a party. She came on hard, as if she had zeroed in on a prize she had to obtain. In retrospect, I suppose that should have scared me a bit, but in truth, I was flattered.

Tracy was petite, pretty, and appeared fragile—a damsel in distress if there ever was one. Within hours we were engrossed in the sad story of her life. She had been mistreated as a child and recently divorced from an abusive man. She solemnly told me about her twelve-month-old son and the horror she faced at the hands of her ex-husband. "He would lock me in the closet for days," she cried. And I believed it. I also believed that she was wild about me. I had no idea she was plotting my demise even back then.

It was kismet. We started dating and she liked everything I liked and appeared almost flawless. This applied to almost everything. For example, she knew I liked country music, so she claimed to like it as well, and only later did I find out that she had never listened to it before. Likewise, she claimed to enjoy wine as I did, when she couldn't stand the stuff. She smooth-talked her way in with my family and friends and would drop subtle hints to them about wanting to be with me. I had thought I found the perfect female companion and never could have imagined that the entire courtship was calculated.

It was a whirlwind relationship, and shortly after we met we were seeing each other frequently. She would drop off her son, Billy, at various friends' homes so we could be alone together, although at the time I thought Billy was with his father. We would go out most evenings each week and then at the end of the evening I would drop her off at her mother's house. She was adamant about never letting me walk her into her home. This was an odd habit that would later be explained by the fact that she wasn't actually staying with her mother.

Tracy was still living with her "abusive" husband. In fact, they weren't even really divorced, although she told me that they were. When I caught her lying about it, the excuses flew out of her mouth more quickly than I could process what she was saying. She told me that she was still living with her husband although she was afraid of him. She said that he locked her in a closet and abused her, but she said she had nowhere else to go because her stepfather had abused her as well. The tears flowed and I was showered with accolades. In the end, it was easier to just believe her. After all, she loved me so much she was willing to lie to be with me.

Oh, the peril of ignoring warning signs.

Tracy has always been controlling and jealous, and often played the victim. I wasn't allowed to see my friends or family because she constantly accused me of using them as cover to see other women. When I worked overtime she would ask to see my paychecks to ensure that I had been working the hours I claimed to be. If I pointed it out to her, she was sometimes able to recognize her jealousy and blame it on her many losses, hardships, and trauma in her life. She said she lacked love and compassion growing up and looked to me as her salvation. She said that my love could heal her and help her to feel better about herself. She begged me to forgive her and to never leave her.

In a sense, she wanted to own me. I was on a very short leash in terms of where I went and who I spent my time with. I would receive an inordinate number of phone calls each day asking me where I was and what I was doing. I found that I was often defending my being anywhere, because she needed to feel that I was in her control. At one of her most frantic moments of jealousy, she crashed a rehearsal dinner I was attending for my friend's wedding to see if I was philandering with any of the women attending. The day of the wedding, Tracy was at the bride's house apologizing for her misbehavior the evening before. She explained that she wanted to keep me all to herself, that she loved me so much she couldn't bear the thought of losing me. This was a trait that, in future years, would carry through in her parenting, with her children becoming her protected possessions.

When she finally left her husband, she and her son, Billy, moved in with me. I was living at my parents' house and she had no problem accepting our help and assistance. In fact, she acted as if she expected it. I worked while she stayed home with her child. I provided her with a new car, a place to stay, and a way to care for Billy. Tracy surprisingly had no qualms about integrating Billy into my family. My parents and I instantly morphed into this child's family, and she appeared to have no remorse for the family she and her son were leaving behind.

Soon after moving in, Tracy let it be known that she was displeased with her new living arrangements. She said that she hated living with my folks. She expressed her desire to have our own house with a yard where we could be a family. And I worked hard to make that happen. We were married and moved into our newly built home later that year.

During that time it wasn't always easy. We started receiving visits from youth and family services over possible abuse of Billy. Billy had stopped growing and his father was concerned that he was being neglected. This was very stressful for Tracy, and she explained that the allegations against her were all her ex-husband's doing. After all, he had been so abusive in the past. She would tell me that he was just jealous and wanted to take her son away. She expressed her wish that I would be Billy's real father, and when the boy started to talk, she coaxed him to call me Daddy. At that time, I had never heard of parental alienation and had no idea it was happening to her ex-husband right in front of me. Worse yet, I was oblivious to the fact that I would be her next victim.

Tracy was extremely manipulative when it came to the father of her child, and she worked hard to ensure that I understood how horrible and abusive he had been to her. She was so successful that, in my mind, this man whom I had never met became the enemy. I did not hear his side of the story until years later, and by then it was too late. At the time, I was working many hours and was often away from home, so many of her court battles with her ex would take place without me knowing about them. Later, when I would receive the lawyer's bills and ask about them, she would offhandedly explain that she had been brought back to court by that "monster." She told me that this man was trying to take her son away from me and I vowed to help her in any way that I could. By that point, I, too, was afraid that the child I had grown to love might be forced to live with his father. The thought of that terrified me and bound Tracy and me together in our fight against this common enemy. It was at the height of this turmoil that we started our own family. She and I had two children together—a son and daughter born two years apart.

They say that the past is the best indicator of future behavior. Shame on me for not being more worried when I witnessed the lack of co-parenting with her first husband. Tracy did not share well with others and that was especially true when it came to her children. She did not seem to believe that a child needs the love and support of both parents; she wanted her children all to herself. She maintained that Billy's father was unfit and could never provide Billy with the things he needed, and I believed her.

Eventually, her first husband remarried and this seemed to make Tracy enraged. If she didn't love him anymore, I didn't see why she should care, but she was furious. Part of what enraged her was that her son now had a stepmother. She seemed to experience this as a competition and she despised sending her son to their house for the weekend. She claimed their home was not safe enough, clean enough, or loving enough. Tracy was convinced that Dana, the new stepmother, was also abusive.

I began to dread their visitation weekends because Tracy would drop Billy off and then fester the entire weekend. She would worry that he wasn't being fed enough or getting enough sleep. She was angry all the time.

As Billy got older, Tracy would pepper him with questions about the time spent at his father's house. She would put her own spin on the stories she heard and called youth and family services on them more than once. A scratch from the family dog became an attack by their vicious pet. If he came home with a stomachache, she would claim he was food poisoned.

As outrageous as her accusations were, I continued to believe her. She was that talented at deceit, and at that point I had no reason to disbelieve or doubt her.

The red flags for my own alienation couldn't have been more vibrant. I was watching parental alienation unfold in front of me with Billy and his father, Tom. Tracy would stop at nothing to "protect" her son from Tom. He would call several times a week to talk to his son and she would always have an excuse to keep father and son apart, claiming that Billy was unavailable. When I would ask what harm there was in letting Billy talk to his dad, I was reminded of the abuse she endured from this man. She told me she hadn't seen a movie in three years because he wouldn't let her out of the house. All she was able to do was cook and clean. When talking about this she would become so distraught that I always found myself relenting and agreeing with her. Obviously, these were facts that would never be proven. I took her word that these things had occurred.

I received a phone call one day from Tom's wife begging me to put an end to Tracy's nonstop harassing. She informed me that their family answering machine would be filled with her daily rants and they had to remove all the machines for their sanity. This was news to me. When I questioned Tracy about this, she clasped her hand to her chest and announced that she would take them back to court for disconnecting the answering machines. She viewed this as a direct attack against her and an attempt to keep her from getting a message to her son, never once recognizing her role in it.

Tracy would never discipline any of our children; this was a job left solely for me. I used to think it was due to her being too delicate to be angry with the kids, but in reality, I think she was playing good cop/bad cop. By design, her role was the fun, easygoing, loving mother, and my role was the heavy ruler with an iron fist. I would often receive calls from her demanding that I punish the children for their wrongdoing the moment I got home. I would figure out years later that after I took away their ice cream or their video games for a week, the kids would turn to her for comfort. She would secretly tell them that she didn't agree with my actions and call me a bully.

The court file on Tracy and Tom's custody case was enormous, and I had a front-row seat to most of it. I had the unfortunate luxury of living in the enemy's camp for fifteen years before she turned on me. I was privy to all of her tricks. I watched the war with Tom play out right in front of me. You would think it would have prepared me for what was ahead, but I was naïve. I thought Tom's treatment was deserved because I believed he was a predator who should be separated from his son. Oh, how my opinion of him changed when similar allegations began to be thrown at me.

It turns out that Tracy is a human chameleon. It is hard to identify her by outward appearance, but she is a dangerous person—all ninety-nine pounds of her. She would use her small size to her advantage, playing the frail victim. And for years it worked; people always felt sorry for her.

No truth is suppressed forever. The truth I came to realize and wish I hadn't was that I married an alienator.

ANNETTE'S STORY

I was nineteen years old when I met John sitting on a train. I was living in New York City at the time as a live-in babysitter at night and a teaching assistant during the day. This was while I was in my second year at college.

I thought he was pleasant looking, so I sat next to him and was aware of his presence on the long ride north from New York. Eventually we struck up a conversation. He was impressed that I was reading an academic book for pleasure (oh, how I was flattered!) and I was impressed that he was older (twenty-four years to my nineteen) and was returning to his high school to lecture on being an actor.

We got along well and arranged to meet on the return trip to New York that Sunday night. We both showed up at the appointed time, settled into the train ride, and got to know each other. At one point he leaned over to kiss me and I was so thrilled that this handsome older man was interested in me. I didn't pay any attention to the fact that I was not particularly interested in him; I was just interested in his being interested in me.

At that point in my life I was feeling quite insecure and uncertain of my future. My mother was in the process of being consumed and defined by her mental illness and made only periodic (and always disturbing) entrances into my life. My father was preoccupied with his revived bachelorhood, and, in my mind, was not particularly interested in making sure that I was okay (in any sense except the most basic). I felt adrift and unsure of my ability to make it in the world. When John showed an interest in me, I felt that I could attach myself to him and I would be taken care of. I wouldn't have to worry about who would take care of me.

John was already divorced from his first wife at that point. He had an apartment in New York and was able to function as an adult. He was a struggling actor, but he managed to make ends meet. John was frugal and hard working and I felt certain that he would always take care of me.

We spent the next few months apart when I returned to college and he remained in New York, but eventually I transferred to a college in the city and moved in with him. By that point he was my anchor and pathway to adulthood, as my family of origin was fragmented. John and I lived together for a few years and then got married. My father footed the bill and John threatened to call off the wedding, and simultaneously increased the expense of the wedding, several times.

My father, in the beginning, was thrilled that John wanted to marry me. I think he felt relief that he could cross me off his list of people to worry about or take care of. It's hard to say looking back whether I loved John or just passively went through the motions of being in the relationship because I didn't have any idea of who I was or what I wanted. I hadn't had any therapy at that point and basically approached the relationship with gratitude that someone wanted me.

On the surface John did seem like the kind of person I would want to be with. He had many positive qualities, such as being hard working, funny, entertaining, upbeat, financially responsible, generous (especially when other people were observing), confident, charming, and competent. He believed that he could pretty much do anything, and with that confidence he approached tasks that other people might have shied away from. I had the sense that he couldn't fail at anything because he wouldn't let himself. Of course, that belief was not consistent with the fact that at twenty-four he was already divorced. I decided to not look too closely at that and believed his version of the story: that he had simply married the wrong person.

All along there were hints of a darker side. At various points in our courtship John became dissatisfied with me and would become extremely cold, angry, and distant. There were times when he did not speak to me for days because of an infraction on my part. During these times I felt as if I did not exist. I was adrift, anchorless, floating through the universe with no sense of myself. When John eventually warmed up to me, I felt nothing so much as intense relief and gratitude. All was once again right in the world.

One of our ongoing sources of tension and conflict was that John flirted with other women and, as an actor, would go away on tour with women— even sharing a room with a woman once. When I expressed my insecurities, he would belittle me and call me derogatory names ("nutsy" being his favorite), and he would let me know that, should he have an affair, it would be my fault because I would have chased him into it with my insecurities. Rather than reassure me that my fears were unnecessary, he actually (purposefully or not) fanned the flames of my doubts and worries.

At some point he had taken to referring to any upset on my part as an indication of my "nutsiness" and would require me to beg him for forgiveness and let him know that I was aware of how damaged I was and how grateful I was for him choosing to stay with me anyway. He let me know that the choice was his and he would stay with me only because he had such a big heart and because he saw something special in me that he felt only he could bring out.

During this period I began to study psychology and became more self-aware. I entered therapy for the first time. This was not easy for John. As he explained it to me one day, I was a weed and he was the gardener, and it was his task to tend to me and help me become a flower. If I entered therapy, it would be like having a different gardener. That would be wrong and unfair to him after all of the effort he had put into taking care of me.

I don't recall now whether I felt insulted at being referred to as a weed, outraged at his self-centeredness and insensitivity, or simply terrified that what I wanted was so threatening to him. I decided to enter therapy anyway, and in response he decided to end the marriage.

Shortly thereafter he called me (I was still living in our apartment, while he was on the road acting) to say that he wanted to reconcile with me, but only if I conceded that none of our marital problems were his fault. I was so relieved that he wanted me back that I readily agreed. Somehow the issue of therapy was not brought up and I continued to go.

After years of trying, I was still not getting pregnant. I wanted to explore medical options, but John was convinced that the reason we didn't conceive was that I was damaged, so there was no point in wasting money on "frivolous" medical procedures. He even refused to have his semen count checked because he took offense at the nurse at the office.

Looking back, I suspect he was afraid to find out that he was the source of the problem. Despite making several thousand dollars a week acting and running a lucrative business, he wouldn't agree to allocate any money to medical tests or adoption. (Needless to say, he was in control of the finances. I still babysat three days a week in order to have my own money.)

Around this time my mother took her own life and at that point John announced to my father that we couldn't have children and couldn't afford to adopt. Looking back, I see that maneuver as a blatant attempt to manipulate my father into giving us money, as we certainly had enough to cover the costs of adoption. In any event, my father thankfully offered us money and John and I proceeded to look into adoption.

To our surprise, our daughter entered our life just three months after my mother died. Before either of us knew it, we were parents. This was to be the most wonderful and the most horrible thing that ever happened to me. Wonderful beyond words, because I loved my daughter so much, and horrible, because of what was to become of my relationship with her.

One of my first memories of being a parent is riding in the backseat with my daughter while John drove us home from the airport. Mia was just two days old. While driving, John looked in the rearview mirror and decided that I was being "nutsy" and proceeded to chide me for being afraid to look at Mia. I suppose I had taken my eyes off of her for a moment and he was already dissatisfied with my parenting. Soon his tune changed, and rather than complaining that I wasn't looking enough, he complained that I loved Mia too much. "You love her more than you love me," he would complain, with no hint of irony or awareness of how childish and narcissistic he sounded.

Over the next three years I tried to stay in the marriage, but in the end it was not tenable. Looking back, I see that all of the elements of the alienation to come were sown during this time.

The first element was his anger and his ability to create a feeling in those around him that they were somehow to blame for his seething discontent. I recall once when my daughter was just two years old and she was playing with the window shade when the thin strip of wood that slides into the bottom of the shade came out. John burst into a tirade against her for not listening to him when he had already told her to not touch the shade. These angry outbursts were not frequent, but when they came were intense and left a lasting fear of what was brewing under the surface.

The second element was his ability to use what I was learning in my psychology classes against me. I had learned a technique in which two adults talk about a child in front of the child as a way to introduce a therapeutic concept in a nonthreatening, indirect manner. John took this technique and would begin speaking to me about my daughter in front of her in a very knowing tone of voice, as if he were speaking the truth. What he was saying was that our daughter was mad at me because I was "being a bad mommy." When our daughter was angry with him he would say to me in front of her, "Mia is mad at Daddy because Mommy is making her be mad at Daddy." The lesson she and I were learning was that everything was my fault.

The third element was the continued devaluing of me. John refused to take pictures of Mia and me together when she was a baby because he said I didn't look good enough. I recall the day I defended my doctoral dissertation. I came home and was holding Mia asleep on my chest. I insisted that he take a photo of us and it is one of the rare pictures of us together at that time.

Another recognizable element was his ability to convince other people (be it our daughter, me, or others) of the rightness of his point of view. John was bright, articulate, and persuasive—even when he was blatantly misinformed or incorrect. He was so convinced of the rightness of his ideas and opinions that it was virtually impossible for him to admit he was wrong or acknowledge that other people had legitimate points of view that could be different. His classic line to me when I said something he didn't agree with was "You are either crazy or lying." I asked him once, "Isn't it possible that I have a legitimate separate perspective?" and his response was a clipped and certain "Nope."

Once our daughter had complained to her daycare provider that her father was tickling her too much. (His physical intrusiveness and aggressiveness were present early on.) The provider shared that information with me (presumably because she didn't feel comfortable telling John directly). I was in the unfortunate position of telling him about the complaint. His response was to sit our daughter down (who was three at the time) and explain to her that it was her job to let him know if he did something she didn't like and that she was being a bad daughter when she wasn't brave enough to do so. John snuggled with her and told her he loved her and held her tightly while he subtly put her down and blamed her. This emotional confusion most likely ended with her feeling badly about herself, rather than comforted and reassured.

Devaluing and cutting off people who upset him was another red flag that was evident throughout our marriage and that would contribute to the alienation. For years John had an on-again, off-again relationship with his brother. When he felt that his brother had slighted him in some way, John would simply stop speaking to him—for months, if not years. He had no qualms about shunning people with whom he was angry (usually because he felt slighted). Once a business partner offended John and from that day forward John stapled the man's monthly check to a piece of paper with about fifty staples, simply to make his life difficult. John relished stapling that check each and every month as he sent his message of hate and revenge through the mail.

No slight was too small to go unpunished. Anyone who cut him off in traffic would get a taste of his own medicine as John would race to pass the person and then dangerously cut him off—regardless of the risk to anyone else in the car. Nothing was more important than punishing the stranger who dared to offend or inconvenience him.

Another important red flag was his inability to cooperate or accommodate the needs of others. When Mia was a baby, he would dunk her head under the water while at our friends' swimming pool. She would come up sputtering and confused. I couldn't stand to see this and more than once begged him not to do it. He insisted that she enjoyed the experience and that it was good for her. Finally I asked him, "Would you be willing to stop just to please me, even though you don't agree that it is bad for her?" He refused. When we were in a marriage counseling session I brought the issue up and he readily agreed to stop when the counselor asked him to. While I was grateful that he wouldn't be engaging in this behavior anymore, I was confused and hurt that he would stop when the counselor asked him to, but not after my repeated requests.

I don't know how I could have thought that I would get out of the marriage unscathed. I don't how I could have dared to hope that we could share our daughter through an amicable divorce. Nonetheless, I had no idea what troubles and sadness awaited me as I became a targeted parent of my precious three-year-old daughter.

SEAN'S STORY

I met my future wife, Sue, while in college. I was in my late teens and was very immature and passive in my approach to relationships. Not knowing what a mentally healthy, two-way relationship was, I naïvely assumed that a good, long marriage would come to me if I said "Yes, dear" to all of my girlfriend's demands and commands. Nearly four years my senior and a former leader in a Christian cult in which we had met, Sue had several advantages in dominating me. My family later said I had gotten out of one cult only to get into another, a personal cult with my wife as the leader. To me it was God's will.

I later learned some things about Sue's childhood that explained her need to dominate and control me, but I was unaware of all of this at the time. She claimed to have been moved thirteen times in twelve years in order to be hidden from her father during a custody battle between her parents. She supposedly lived in fear during her formative years due to investigators going through their garbage. There was a backstory of ongoing litigation involving my wife and her family of origin. She had been in a lawsuit against an employer for an injury on the job, and her family was also pursuing a right-to-die case for her maternal grandfather against a Catholic hospital that had heroically resuscitated him, supposedly against his wishes. My mother-in-law was on Phil Donahue's show about the case. I was unaware of all this at the time and, based on my wife's assertions alone, can't be sure what is true.

Sue certainly portrayed herself to me as having a difficult childhood, joking that I was a "sucker" for a hard-luck case in wanting to marry her. Truth be told, marriage was the farthest thing from my mind. She fabricated my intentions to marry her by misconstruing a holiday card I had sent her (and all the other college kids in our church's campus ministry) over one Christmas break. With literally only two weeks of "dating," Sue kept me up all night with long discussions designed to elicit a marriage proposal from me. With little dating experience, I was in the middle of a college degree program and had no intention of looking for a spouse. I was pursuing my dreams in music performance, and not looking for a family and job to take me away from what I had worked so hard to accomplish by getting into the school I was attending. But Sue prevailed, and before I knew it, she was planning our wedding. For a wedding song, she chose "Since You Asked," although, in all honesty, I had not been the one asking, or even volunteering. Rather, I was the one being "voluntold."

I shocked my mom and family by calling up one day out of the blue to announce my engagement to someone they didn't know and had not been told anything about. Sue insisted on a date for the wedding that prevented my best man from attending an annual event in Washington, DC, that he hadn't missed for years and made it extremely difficult for my twin sister to attend during her final exams. Thus began my alienation from my family. My wife created situations in which I felt obligated to choose her over my family, resulting in their feeling hurt and angry with me. My mother responded by cutting me off financially since I was getting married without her blessing.

To make matters worse, around this time Sue instituted a rule that neither of us would speak to our families without the other present. My personal phone calls and e-mails had become my wife's business. No further communications were made without her present and listening. Sometimes Sue even insisted on taking over the conversations for me. Later I found out that she routinely had private calls and e-mails with her family unbeknownst to me. "Our" rules, evidently, only applied to me.

While I was still in college, Sue decided "we" would use the symptothermal method of birth control, which relies on tracking the woman's temperature to determine when to refrain from sex. I recall a school buddy of mine laughing when I told him about this, saying that we'd be expecting within the year! Sure enough, we were expecting a child before we had agreed on starting our family.

With the impending arrival of our first child, Sue insisted upon an elaborate birth plan detailing who would be included in the birthing suite. She then proceeded to disregard the plan by inviting her mother and stepfather, without discussing it with me. I would not have minded their involvement, had it not been for the big deal my wife made about the birthing plan and what happened next: my in-laws chose to stand on either side of my wife during the last part of her labor, physically displacing me from my wife's side during the birth of our first child. At the time, I was exhausted from being up several days with Sue while she was monitored and had labor induced, and I was too tired to do anything but accept what she wanted.

At the time I felt emotionally squashed. My efforts to bring up my problem with what had happened were met with my wife's disapproval, leading me to acquiesce once again. This became the pattern of our relationship. I had gotten used to being manipulated by her, or, as my attorney later observed, "accustomed to abnormal."

Another interesting aspect of this whole event was that Sue was disappointed that her due date came and went with no labor in sight. She took things into her own hands and deliberately ate salty foods to raise her blood pressure and hence make her eligible to be hospitalized and have labor induced. I was unaware of this ploy and only accidentally discovered it, as she had clearly meant to keep it a secret, even from me. This was not the last time that she would do this.

Following our first son's birth, we lost twins whom we tried hard to save by having my wife on strict bed rest during the pregnancy. I remember washing her hair over a plastic sheet into a bucket as she lay on the couch. I tried to tend to her every need. In retrospect, the only source of information about what was happening to my wife and our unborn babies was my wife. To this day, I am not sure of what actually happened in this or many other instances in our life together, because all information came solely from her and was only allegedly corroborated by people who could not be reached by anyone other than my wife.

We lost the twins while I was in basic military training, and my wife, on her own, elected to be induced and have a stillbirth. She did this without letting me know, but that did not stop her from later complaining that nobody sympathized with her loss, and that the military had not let me join her for the labor and delivery. Devastated and in the dark, I accepted what Sue relayed to me.

Our second child was born in a midwifery center, and his arrival was a better experience for me. There was no elaborate birthing plan and no extended family to displace me from my wife's side. However, I was put in a no-win situation by Sue in that she wanted some things from our car, and yet was angry for months after that because I had left her—at her request—to fetch these items. It seemed that I could not do anything right when it came to her and our children. She was the expert, and she was not to be contradicted.

When our third and final child was born, two doulas (birthing helpers) whom my wife arranged to have by her side were there—again without asking what I wanted. By this point in our marriage, I accepted whatever she wanted without question. This time, it was two women I didn't know, holding her hand, stroking her hair, and fetching whatever she desired. According to my wife, this was the best birthing experience "we" had.

Over the years, I noticed that my wife would research the symptoms of a medical condition in order to create the impression that she or the children had that condition when that was not the case. She would be sure to mention the symptoms during the examination in order to ensure the doctor wouldn't miss the signs and fail to prescribe medicine or order a procedure that my wife had already decided was necessary. This tactic was used by her over the years and was especially effective sixteen years later, after we had been married about twenty years, when she studied a brochure from a battered women's shelter, noting the signs of abuse. She included this information in a false complaint against me, without even bothering to change the order of the symptoms listed on the brochure. This was done through an ex parte restraining order, which allowed her to eventually abduct our three children.

I see now that there were so many red flags as to the type of uncooperative co-parent my wife would turn out to be. It is incredible that I didn't see at the time what kind of person she was. Admittedly, I was not mature enough to know what to do even if I had wanted to get out of the marriage. The marriage happened so fast and I believed I had made a commitment that could not be broken. My worldview led me to conclude that it must have been God's will, or it would not have happened. Thus, I fell prey to her, and only years later came to understand the dynamics between us.

Can I say she is ill? No. Can I say she is evil? No. All I can say is that I forgive her and that I long for the return of my loving relationship with our three children. My wife got (and still gets) whatever she wants from me. Nearly my entire paycheck goes to her, even eight years later. Her whole sense of self seems to come from being the parent of children devoted exclusively to her. To achieve her goal, she adopted the self-created fictitious role as a heroic battered wife who freed herself and her three children from an emotional tyrant, triumphantly raising them on her own.

Many little things flood back to mind when I consider how I could possibly have come to suffer the nightmare of a life I currently endure—being violently and completely cut off from my three children. One thing I recall is a game my wife used to play. She would place her hands all over the kids and say, "All mine; all Momma's." This seemed innocent at the time, but disturbing in light of her ultimate abduction of them.

I also recall one occasion when she wrote me a love letter praising me for cutting my mother out of our lives. She was so happy that I chose her over my mother. My wife claimed that I "misbehaved" after calls with my mother, as if I were a child. I reasoned that my wife had to come first in a healthy marriage. In order to make peace with my wife, I told my mother that we didn't want any more of her visits or calls (just her money when we were in trouble), and we were going to restrict our contact with her to letter writing. In her love letter to me, my wife explained how she felt more attracted to me than ever. Why didn't I see at the time how unhealthy this was? It is clear as day to me, now.

The physician she went to shortly before she left with the children told me that she was abusing the children. I was also told by a therapist she had seen, but refused to go back to, that she was seriously mentally ill and I would be lucky to be away from her. There is some truth to that. I am happily remarried for four years now, with a normal woman and a beautiful stepdaughter who loves me. I keep making myself the best person I can be so that my children have someone worth returning to. I didn't know how good life could be! The only pain now is that of the deep, unhealed wounds from the loss of my children I am currently enduring and may never see rectified this side of heaven.

I maintain the belief that everything happens for a reason, and I hold on to hope that I will eventually be joyously reunited with my children and they will get the help they will so desperately need based on the upbringing they received. I am living for that day.

MARIE'S STORY

I met Jack when we both were eighteen years old. We lived in Paris at the time. During the two years of friendship and seven years of living together prior to getting married, there were plenty of bright red flags that I chose to ignore. I was inexperienced in love and so I married him. I loved him but now realize that love is definitely not enough: When only one partner makes all the compromises, looks the other way, and bends over backward to please the other, the relationship is off-balance. Ours was like that from the beginning. He was intelligent, charismatic, the leader of the pack of friends, and the decision maker. He always had his way.

I can see now that his personality style would make parenting with him a challenge. But at the time I didn't look at his flaws with the parenting perspective in mind. I also didn't realize that many of his personality traits were indicative of narcissism, which would have long-term implications for our relationship. At the time I labeled them "caveman/macho/egomaniac" when I was frustrated with his behavior.

Back in the early 1980s, we had already been living together for a couple of years. Instead of finding work in the corporate world, he wanted to write books and be famous. After a few months as a journalist, he did find someone who would publish his books. (She was fifteen years older than him and became his mistress for four years, which helped.) He would handwrite his manuscripts, and I would type them for him because I was a faster typist than he. I did the typing at night in the bathroom so that he could sleep or watch TV. At that point I was also working full-time. I am still trying to figure out how I could let him take advantage of me that way.

I also remember times when I would be trying to get some sleep so I wouldn't be tired at work the next day, and he would stay up late at night watching TV. He didn't seem to care when I asked him to turn it off. He would turn it down a little, but not off. I never found a way to voice my frustration, and I was letting myself be trained to want to please him, because I loved him.

We were "an item," and being with him gave me stature. I am more on the quiet side, and I enjoyed shining through him. I was proud to be with him. I was afraid of losing him, so I didn't try to get my needs met. I did this in the name of love.

Eight years after we started dating I asked him to stop seeing other people. We had moved to the United States and I felt that I needed that kind of commitment from him. After finally confronting him about the other woman he had been seeing for four years, I told him to go away with her and give that relationship a real try. He agreed and they moved away together. Although I felt sad, I also felt free. And while Jack was supposed to be in a serious relationship with her, he would still try to be intimate with me when I was in town for work. Eventually, she broke up with him and I took him back.

He told me that he had found God and I assumed that this meant he would respect the sanctity of marriage and wouldn't cheat on me anymore. We got married but he wanted to keep it quiet, so I didn't tell my parents for three months. We married on a weekday, at the courthouse, by the justice of the peace, with his secretary as a witness. We went to have lunch and I went to work that afternoon. No engagement ring, no party —but I was happy.

We moved back to France and for the next eighteen months things were picture perfect. He was a new man. He was engaged in his faith, he was the perfect husband, caring, we had many friends—it was dreamy. I was thirty-two and got pregnant. We came back to the States because he wanted to obtain an MBA. Each time we moved, I left my life and work behind and went with him. This time I was pregnant.

I was the only caregiver of our three children. In all the years, he didn't change five diapers, didn't attend one doctor's visit, didn't arrange for baby-sitters, didn't find schools. He missed the first day of pre-K drama; he missed all the school performances. He never helped the children learn to read or do their homework; he never organized playdates or birthday parties, never shopped for their birthday or Christmas presents; he never read bedtime stories, never comforted them after a nightmare; he never took them to the park or helped them learn to ride their bike or learn to swim.

I could go on and on. He missed it all, and I was blessed to do all of it when my children were growing up, because nobody can ever take that away from me. I certainly would have appreciated some support here and there. Absolutely. When I would ask for help, his favorite answer would be "I don't know how to do that," or "I don't have the time," or "It is a woman's job." He always had an excuse, so it come to a point at which it was easier for me to do it rather than argue and ending up doing it all anyway.

That is not to say that he didn't love them. I think he did. But he was also jealous of the attention and time I was dedicating to them. Ironically, he failed to understand that if he had helped me with the kids, I would have had more time to dedicate to him. What I was beginning to understand was that I

needed to be very careful around Jack, or else he would become very angry
with me, even over seemingly minor events such as a letter getting lost or a
car battery dying.

Jack was very insistent that he was always right. When our son was in
pre-K, Jack wanted him to enter first grade at five years, as he had when he
was growing up. The school required a psychologist assessment, and I agreed
partly because I realized there was no use going against Jack, and also because I had become proud of having such an advanced child. It turned out to
be a very bad decision and our son suffered throughout that first grade year. I
remember his teacher reaching out to me to share that he was having a hard
time adjusting to the schoolwork because he wanted to play. He was also
having a hard time engaging with the other children who were a year or more
older than him. To this day I know this was a terrible decision that impacted
him for many years.

Now I see that it was not about what was best for our son, but about what
would make Jack feel good about himself. He could showcase the fact that
his son entered first grade at just five years of age. Over all of the years when
the issue would come up, Jack never acknowledged that it was a mistake that
our son paid for. I don't recall his ever admitting he made a mistake about
anything, although he was keen to point out all of mine.

As the kids were growing up, our marital relationship deteriorated. We
had good moments, but overall it was going downhill. Jack was unable to
provide financially for the family. He was self-employed but in my opinion
didn't apply himself. I made the terrible mistake of working for him, and for
the eighteen years that I did so, he treated me like his employee, secretary,
travel agent, busboy, and so forth. When he was an attorney he expected me
to be his secretary, organizing his documents, filing motions, running to the
courthouse. Whenever I wanted some time to take care of the kids, house,
and so on, he would play the guilt card, saying, "By helping me at work you
are helping the family!"

In 1997, when he ran for Congress, our house became the Grand Central
Station of his political allies, supporters, and campaign manager. Not only
was this incredibly stressful, but we also lost a lot of money. It also seemed
to bring out paranoia in him, as he became obsessed with certain people
whom he claimed had it in for him.

I got pregnant during the campaign. At the first sonogram appointment I
learned that the fetus was not alive, and I was scheduled to go to the hospital
the next day. When I told Jack, he asked, "Do you need me?" I paused, and

then calmly answered, "No." I left early by myself, dropped the children off at school and went to the hospital. Inside I had been hoping that he would know that I needed him to be with me and that he would want to be there for me. But that was not to be. He probably slept in that day, like every other day. My mother and my sister came to visit me. I came home that same day and was right back on the campaign trail for him, again.

In the spring of 2004, Jack insisted we move to New York to escape his political enemies. I was concerned about how the children would fare in American schools, being expected to speak English and adapt to a new life. They were thirteen, nine, and six at the time. Once again, I left my family, my friends, and my job to follow him. He didn't seem to care that I did not want this move. As before, I did all of the preparation: I found the new house, I found the new schools, I did all of the packing and arranging for storage, and more than I want to remember. I dedicated myself to helping the kids get settled in this new life of theirs.

By this point I had no work and Jack had no work and we were totally dependent on our savings. In the meantime, he was traveling back and forth every other month, staying in Europe for weeks at a time wrapping up loose ends and trying to maintain political allegiances. The sad part is that the tension between us had become such that even though I was lonely, I preferred it when he was away. Then Jack decided to return to school, to get a United States law degree. This became his total focus and thus the focus of the family for the next several years to come. In 2010, everything came to a head with his failing the bar: we lost our home and the pressure was too much. After much deliberation and great sadness I told Jack that I wanted a divorce. I thought that was the end of my misery, but really it was just the beginning.

Chapter Three

If I Knew Then What I Know Now

In reading Marty's, Sean's, Marie's, and Annette's stories, it is easy to see—with the advantage of hindsight—that these marriages were doomed from the start. In this chapter the common themes across these stories are discussed. These themes were also evident in the many other stories submitted for this book as well. One way to think about the early relationships between the future targeted parents and the future alienators is that they represent a kind of perfect storm comprised of

1. an insecure and/or naïve person who doesn't know him-/herself that well seeking reassurance and acceptance from a more experienced or knowledgeable partner,
2. a charming manipulator, and
3. the warning signs that begged for recognition, but were ignored.

THE FUTURE TARGETED PARENT

The Perils of Youth: Lack of Experience Detecting Manipulators

The future targeted parents at the time he or she became involved with the future alienator, appear to have been young, naïve, and insecure. Annette, Sean, Marie, and others who submitted stories were in their late teens or early twenties when they met their future spouse. Youth in and of itself is not a problem except that it represents a lack of experience with relationships in general, and particularly with people who present themselves as loving, honest, caring, and committed but are actually selfish, deceitful, controlling, and manipulative. Only sufficient exposure to a number of different people and exposure to each one of these people over an extended period of time would provide someone with the opportunity to be aware of the discrepancies between how a person presents him-/herself and who she or he truly is. In essence, the future targeted parents were novices at relationships. This is exemplified by a submission for this book in which a woman wrote, "Tim was twenty-eight and I was twenty-two. I was taken with him. . . . He had a great job as a policeman, his own beautiful log house. He took me on my first airplane ride, took me out to eat a lot and shopping. He seemed like a dream." She didn't know that her dream would one day become a nightmare. How could she? As a novice, she assumed that Tim was who he said he was: a decent person who would be a loving and faithful husband.

One way that novices and experts in any field are differentiated is that experts have a depth and breadth of experience that allows them to engage in what is known as "pattern recognition." An experienced doctor who has seen many patients in his long career will be able to observe the signs and symptoms presented by a new patient and match those signs relatively quickly to a particular disease pattern that the doctor has already observed. He can match the symptoms with the right disease because he recognizes the pattern of symptoms from his prior experience. He has a greater number of patterns in his head from which to choose, so it is more likely that he will choose the right one (and disregard the wrong ones). The novice doctor, however, will have access to fewer patterns from which to choose based on his more limited exposure over a shorter career. In the same vein, a young adult just beginning to date will most likely have limited prior experience dating a charming manipulator and may therefore not recognize one until it feels as if it is too late to get out of the relationship.

Being young also means having less experience reading the internal warning signs that may be going off, less experience trusting one's "gut." As one woman who also submitted her story wrote about an older man she had met, "We dated for a while, during which time there were several occasions when my 'gut' told me that there was just something not right with this guy. But I told myself I must be wrong. After all, he was a professional and others at work respected him." This young woman simply did not have enough life experience to know that she should trust those internal feelings.

In the absence of life experience, the novice may well have been drawn to a relationship pattern that was familiar: the one he or she had experienced with his or her own parents. For some future targeted parents, there may have been an attraction to a future alienator who was reminiscent of his or her own parents and thus was all too familiar—but unfortunately not in a good way.

In general, our parents provide a template for what relationships should feel like. When we meet someone "just like" Mom or Dad, that person can feel right and therefore may be difficult to resist. Even if the similarity comes from negative qualities such as being controlling and abusive, that future mate will "feel right," despite being all wrong. This is particularly true if the future targeted parent has not been in psychotherapy or otherwise engaged in an examination of the impact of his or her own family of origin on his or her choices and behavior. Again, being young means self-examination would be less likely. This might be one reason that John wanted to keep Annette out of therapy, fearing that the process would open her eyes in ways that would be inconvenient to him. At age nineteen, Annette did not have enough self-knowledge or life experience to understand that what felt like a good match was in fact a disaster waiting to happen.

Naïve/Gullible

There are many definitions of gullible, but the essence of each describes being easily misled to believe things that others would easily know were false. That certainly describes the future targeted parents who wrote their stories for this book. None of them appeared to suspect that their future spouse was lying or deceiving them, even when there were obvious signs. They were unworldly and trusting and didn't suspect that the other person was anything other than who they said they were. This might just be a function of their youth and inexperience, or it might be a quality of their personality (trusting by nature), or both.

Annette shared a story about her future alienator, John, who had her convinced that there was a man on Lexington Avenue who personally made double-stuffed Oreo cookies for him. This was a story he told early in their relationship, and it is possible that John was testing the degree of Annette's gullibility—in the same way that a sexual predator will "groom" a future victim by slowly violating physical boundaries to determine how far the child will let him go and to acclimate the child to incrementally increasing violations. This kind of child molester doesn't just grab the child out of the blue, because that would most likely set off warning bells in the child. Instead, he will lightly touch or tickle the child or give him a bear hug to see how the child responds. Likewise, the charming manipulator may tell an innocuous little fib to see whether he or she will get called on it. If the fib is not caught, the future alienator has learned that the future targeted parent is gullible and will most likely not be suspicious of the future alienator in the future. John learned important information about Annette when he told her about the cookies: she was not worldly and would be likely to believe almost anything he told her. He would use this knowledge throughout their marriage and divorce. Likewise, Tracy learned from lying to Marty about where she was living. When the truth came out, he chose to ignore the inconsistencies in her explanations as long as she showered him with flattery and confused him with dramatic displays of emotions. From this she learned how to keep him in the relationship as long as it suited her needs.

Low Self-Esteem

The future targeted parents also seem to share the quality of being insecure, lacking in a strong sense of their worth and their right to be treated with kindness, honesty, and respect. They seemed to be missing the automatic self-protective response of anger or indignation that some people have when treated badly. In reading these stories it is hard not to marvel at what these future targeted parents put up with from their mates. Think of Marie slaving away at night typing her boyfriend's papers while he lounged in the next room watching television, or Sean being pushed aside during the birth of his children while others doted on and tended to his wife. Both stories (and many others we read) reveal a brazen lack of respect for the rights and feelings of the future targeted parent, a clear sign that the future alienator did not value and respect the future targeted parent's dignity.

In one story, a man told about how, early in their relationship, his future wife "gave me a Three Stooges sort of slap to the back of the head, as if to say 'You're a bit of an idiot.'" He reported that he was "a bit shocked" but chose to "let it ride." He continues: "Not five minutes later Janice did the exact same thing, laughing and smiling like she was the life of the party." A pattern emerged in their relationship in which Janice disregarded her husband's feelings, something she learned would be accepted based on his early response to her behavior when he choose to "let it ride."

It is important to note that the future targeted parent benefited in some ways from the relationship despite the negative aspects. The future targeted parents spoke of feeling flattered, special, and elevated by being chosen by the future alienator. They gained a boost to their egos when the older, more worldly, or in some way more desirable and attractive person chose them. At least at first.

For some future targeted parents, attaching themselves to the seemingly more desirable future alienator gave them a (false) sense of increased belonging and worth. One woman who submitted her story began what seems to be a familiar sounding theme: "Wally and I met at my first job out of college. I was young and a new employee at a consulting firm, and he was an older, more experienced project manager. I looked up to him professionally, and thought that others did as well." She perceived him to be an esteemed person with power and prestige at her job and felt lucky that he turned his attention to her. Likewise, Marie wrote about her relationship with Jack, "I enjoyed shining through him. I was proud to be with him."

Shining through someone may be exciting and reassuring at first, but—as the saying goes—all that glitters is not gold. Because Marie's sense of worth and purpose was derived externally from Jack, rather than internally from her own authentic self, she was in a relationship with a significant power imbalance (as were the other future targeted parents). She needed Jack in order to feel good about herself. Marie and the other future targeted parents had in a sense handed over their power to the future alienator who could—through disapproval and rejection—revoke the future targeted parent's sense of worth and purpose. It is no wonder that the future targeted parents feared rejection and abandonment by the future alienator. Not only would the relationship be lost, but so would their sense of worth and value.

Coming from this one-down position, the future targeted parents allowed the future alienators to exercise undue control in most, if not all, aspects of their relationship. The future targeted parents needed the relationship more than they needed anything else, so they were willing to give up almost anything else in order to maintain the relationship.

A man who submitted his story for the book told how his girlfriend broke up with him, told others that he had abused her, and then suddenly reappeared after two years. He says, "The relationship picked up quickly from where it left off. We had no meaningful discussions as to what happened previously, or why. I had missed her, and was willing to let past mistakes remain buried." That willingness would get him into a lot of trouble later, but in the moment that they were reconciling, he only felt gratitude that she had deigned to accept him back into her life.

That willingness to let things ride is echoed throughout the stories. The future targeted parents allowed the future alienators to control the family finances, to dictate where the family would live, to determine which schools the children would attend, as well as most, if not all, of the major decisions that affected the marriage and the family. Sean's wife, for example, decided unilaterally to terminate her pregnancy.

In another submission the author recounted how his wife declared that she wanted to terminate her pregnancy by grabbing her pregnant belly and yelling, "I can kill him anytime I want and there's nothing you can do about it!" Later, when the child died shortly after childbirth, she had him cremated without conferring with the father. In another submission, a woman told how—while house hunting—her husband announced to the realtor without any discussion with his wife that he was prepared to make an offer on the house. She wrote, "The realtor was shocked and asked if we wanted some time to go to dinner and discuss things. We did go to dinner, but there was no discussion because Tim had made the decision." This woman didn't feel that she could have a voice in this or any other decisions affecting her family.

Some of the future targeted parents also put up with imposed limits on their relationships with their own friends and families. For example, one man wrote, "I was not allowed to go anywhere with any of my single friends because she did not trust me. I was not allowed to have my own e-mail account if she was not allowed access to it." The future alienators instituted rules about how much contact there could be and when the contact would take place. In one extreme case, Sean's wife insisted that he choose between his family and her. In another submission, a woman writes, "As the children grew, Frank continued to give me difficulty with outings with family and friends. He would get very cold and distant when I would want to do anything with them. It got so that I didn't even like to ask Frank if I could go. I started giving excuses for not attending family outings and invites from friends."

In this sense, the future targeted parents lived like victims of domestic abuse in which their spouse systematically cut them off from friends and family. They had fewer people in their lives to challenge the status quo and to question the attitudes and behaviors of the future alienator. There were fewer people to say, "This is not okay," and "You don't need to take this." It seemed as if, without such a reminder, they did not believe that they deserved better.

In *Stop Controlling Me!*, psychologist Richard Stenack explores why some people allow other people to control them. "At the heart of the problem is a sense of inadequacy, a lack of faith in your own okayness," he writes, and this seems to be the case for many future targeted parents.[1] If they didn't feel "okay" with themselves, they would be more likely to rely on the future alienator to decide whether they were okay. And as Stenack argues, "If you must rely on someone else to tell you that you're okay, you're in trouble."[2] The future targeted parents were certainly in trouble.

According to Stenack, what an insecure person is most afraid of is rejection, because rejection is experienced as confirmation of inferiority. To avoid what feels like a catastrophic event, the insecure person will go to any lengths to avoid being rejected. "The simplest way to avoid being rejected is by not showing another person anything that might be an excuse for rejection. That means more than anything else, not showing how you feel about things—or even showing that you have feelings."[3]

Denial: What Red Flags?

For the future targeted parents it went beyond not *showing* how they felt to actually not *knowing* how they felt. Their low self-esteem, coupled with their naïveté and youth, seems to have led them to squash their own questions and concerns about the relationship. They didn't allow themselves to know the truth that eventually became too obvious for them to ignore, and because they were being cut off from their friends and family, there were fewer people to whom they could turn to discuss their doubts and to examine the relationship from other points of view.

At the outset of the relationship, however, they chose to ignore the red flags. It was more important to preserve the relationship than to know and speak the truth. And to some extent, the situation itself also called for a certain amount of dismissal of the red flags. As psychologist and relationship expert Bethany Marshall notes in her book *Deal Breakers: When to Work on a Relationship and When to Walk Away*, "Romantic relationships require optimism, hope, and idealization to get off the ground. Because of this, important warning signs can easily be ignored."[4] And yet, as psychologist Harriet Lerner observes in *The Dance of Connection*, "Falling in love tells us absolutely nothing about whether a particular relationship is healthy or good for us."[5]

According to another psychologist and relationship expert, Barbara DeAngelis, future targeted parents are not alone in ignoring warning signs.[6] She points out in her book *Are You the One for Me?* that of the six common "big mistakes" that people make when dating, one is to ignore the warning signs of potential problems. She says this happens in at least four ways:

1. Minimizing the importance of the questionable behavior (e.g., "It is not that bad that she hits me in the back of the head.")
2. Making excuses for the other person (e.g., "He doesn't mean to hurt my feelings when he flirts with other women; he is just being friendly.")
3. Rationalizing away the problematic behavior (e.g., "I am a better typist, so it makes sense that I should type Jack's papers for him.")
4. Denying the existence of the problem (e.g., "Tracy must be so upset for some reason. So what if the facts don't add up; she was probably abused by her ex in some way.")

These other "big mistakes" were also common among the future targeted parents:

1. Not asking enough questions (e.g., Annette and Marty chose not to look too closely at their spouses' former marriages)
2. Making premature compromises (e.g., Sean allowed himself to be pressured into a marriage proposal he didn't really want to make)
3. Assuming that chemistry meant love (e.g., Marty believed that the feeling of kismet indicated that he and Tracy were meant for each other)
4. Giving in to material seduction (e.g., Annette was looking for someone to take care of her)
5. Putting commitment before compatibility (e.g., it was more important for Marie to be in a relationship than it was that Jack share her belief in fidelity)

In a sense, the future targeted parents decided that the relationship was right for them and then made the facts fit that picture rather than seeing the facts for what they were and understanding what story the facts were really telling them. DeAngelis says, "Most people put more time and effort into deciding what kind of car or video player to buy than they do in deciding whom to have a relationship with."[7] And it does seem that the future targeted parents who told their stories for this book put little effort into consciously deciding whether they wanted these relationships. She also points out that many people end up in relationships for the "wrong reasons," and again, these seem to apply to the future targeted parents: pressure, loneliness, sexual hunger, distraction from life, avoiding growing up, guilt, or needing to fill emotional/spiritual emptiness. If a person decides that they want a relationship no matter what, then they will be highly motivated to ignore the warning signs, no matter how glaring.

Because they were young, naïve, and inexperienced, they did not approach the relationship from a place of personal power. They did not appear to be to asking themselves, "Is this the kind of relationship that I want?" According to Bethany Marshall, "In order to spot a deal breaker, you must first have a deal. By this, I mean you must know what you hope to get out of the relationship."[8] Because the future targeted parents did not define for themselves what they wanted from the relationship—other than to have the relationship—they were willing to put up with almost anything, even qualities that "eroded their most cherished aspirations for a satisfying love relationship."[9] They were living with what many people would consider "deal breakers," conditions that make it impossible to feel accepted and loved.

And once in the relationship, it seems that it was very hard for them to get out, even after the warning signs started to become more obvious. This is a common psychological phenomenon in which bad decisions are maintained. To change one's mind would be like "turning a steamship around in a narrow river," as distinguished psychologists Carol Tavris and Eliot Aronson explain in their latest book, *Mistakes Were Made (But Not by Me)*.[10] The psychological commitment that the future targeted parents felt for the relationship kept them in it long after the relationship stopped working for them.

THE FUTURE ALIENATOR AS A SPOUSE

Confusing the Issue: Intentional Deceit

Added to this mix is the intentional deceit and manipulation of the future alienator. While the future targeted parent might have been naïve, inexperienced, and gullible, the future alienators were anything but. They tended to be older (by comparison) and more advanced in their careers and life experiences, having had prior marriages and sometimes children. They were also able to hide or deflect attention away from the more obvious signs of their underlying deviousness until the relationship had been solidified. Deceitful and manipulative people are able to mimic normal behavior—especially in the beginning of a relationship. They can, in fact, appear quite attentive, warm, responsive, and sensitive.

Many of these individuals spoke about feeling wonderful, loved, and attended to in the beginning of the relationship. They said things like "It was a dream," "It was dreamy," "It was kismet," and "It was a whirlwind high of emotions for me," or even "He just swept me off my feet." The future alienators were able to make the future targeted parents feel special and wonderful, at least for a while. By the time the future targeted parents noticed that the tides had turned, it was too late.

In the book *In Sheep's Clothing*, clinical psychologist George K. Simon observes that some people are very clever at masking their efforts to control another person.[11] Thus it may not have been obvious, at least at first, that control and manipulation were occurring. The strategies that Simon identifies as common among "wolves" are prevalent among the future alienators we heard about. First, they use obfuscation to make it difficult for the other person to see what is really going on. That is, they were not transparent or obvious in their efforts to deceive and control. Think, for example, about how Marty never did get a clear story about whether Tracy's ex-husband was abusive. How could Marty know what really happened when, every time he brought it up, Tracy became distraught and sobbed hysterically? The "noise" she made emotionally distracted Marty from his question and brought the attention back to Tracy's distress and pain. Rather than getting answers, he got tears. Rather than holding her accountable, he held her and comforted her. Similarly, Annette stopped asking John about his rooming situation while touring out of town because she would receive a full dose of anger and threats in response. She became so distracted with fear that John would be disappointed in her that she forgot her initial concern and her intention to discuss it with him.

A second tactic is the use of deception to evade getting caught. When confronted with an apparent discrepancy, the manipulative future alienators lied in order to avoid having their original deception exposed. Tracy claimed to be too afraid to divorce her husband and too much in love with Marty to tell him the truth. She did not come clean and simply admit that she had taken liberties with the truth; she told Marty that she was divorced and living with her mother, when in fact she was married and living with her husband.

Third, wolves in sheep's clothing know how to exploit the other person's weaknesses and insecurities. In order to gain the advantage in the relationship and exercise their control, they prey on the other person's fear of abandonment, fear of anger, or inability to stand up for themselves. Every time John referred to Annette as "nutsy," he was reinforcing the idea that she was damaged and that he might decide that she was too much trouble for him. By insulting her and labeling her, he was reinforcing her fear that he might leave her. Marie's desire for her son to be considered gifted by others allowed her to be misled by Jack into pressuring the school to promote the child when he wasn't ready. When Marie questioned why Jack was asking her to do his secretarial work on top of everything else, he would doubt her devotion to the family and prey on her fear that she wasn't a good enough wife. In that way he kept her both in line and doing his work—making his life easier, no matter the inconvenience to her.

The final "wolf" strategy is to recast the questionable behavior as a result of pain and suffering rather than a reflection of selfishness, deceit, and inconsideration. The future targeted parent was encouraged by the future alienator to view the problematic behavior as a sign of their pain in order to invoke "understanding" and pity rather than the deserved outrage. Tracy, for example, played on Marty's love and concern for her by playing the wounded victim, rather than appearing as the deceitful manipulator that she was.

Power and Control Strategies

Intentional deceit is one way to maintain control, but there are others as well. One woman who submitted a story explained that her husband said that he would make the major decisions for the family, "because a family is riding in a car and only one person could be at the wheel." Another wrote that her husband "explained his many rules with complete certainty in their rightness and logic. . . . He seemed so rational, so smart. I didn't have the confidence in myself to argue." Dr. Simon and domestic violence expert Lundy Bancroft[12] each identify numerous specific tactics that manipulators use to maintain their power and control in their relationships. It is easy to see the applicability to the stories presented by the participants in this book. In table 3.1 each type is listed, along with an explanation and a hypothetical example based on the stories.

THE FOUR HORSEMEN OF THE APOCALYPSE

John Gottman, one of the country's leading researchers on what makes marriages work and the author of *Why Marriages Succeed or Fail*, has identified four qualities (the four horseman of the apocalypse) that differentiate marriages that are "masters" from those that are "disasters."[13] The marital disasters are headed for certain discord and likely divorce. Looking at just a "thin slice" of a marital interaction, as defined by Malcolm Gladwell in *Blink*,

Table 3.1. Manipulation Tactics

Type of Behavior	Explanation	Examples
Minimizing	Saying that his or her behavior isn't really that bad or harmful (as someone else is saying), trivializing the wrongdoing or the impact on others	"What are you so upset about?" "Why do you have to spoil the fun?" "I was starting to feel really close to you and then you have to ruin it with your complaints."
Lying by Omission	Leaving out important details that change the meaning of what is being said	"I didn't tell you about the party because I knew you would get all upset and make a big deal out of nothing."
Denying	Refusing to admit when he or she has done something harmful, refusing to admit the motivation behind the behaviors, or refusing to admit having a hidden agenda	"I did not flirt with that other woman; you just can't take a joke. I was just fooling around."
Attending Selectively	Actively ignoring warnings and pleas or wishes of others	"You never told me that you needed me home. How was I supposed to know?"
Rationalizing	Making excuses to engage in what he or she knows is harmful behavior, allowing him or her to remove internal resistance	"All I did was move the money from one account to another so I could get a better rate. What's the problem with that?"
Diverting Attention	Changing the subject, keeping the focus off of his or her own behaviors and hidden agendas, keeping the other person on the defensive	"If you didn't get so upset all of the time, I would have told you that I was going away for the weekend, but I hate to hear you make such a fuss. It's your own damn fault."
Evading Detection	Giving rambling, incoherent, and vague responses to appear as if he or she is being compliant and responsive, but not really being so	"You see, it's like this. I hear about this terrific offer from my buddy and you are always ragging on me for not being enough of a go-getter, so I decided that . . ."
Intimidating Subtly	Keeping others in a one-down position so as not to be challenged or required to change	"If I have an affair, it will be your fault because your insecurity will chase me away. Don't blame me if it happens."

Provoking Guilt	Using the conscientiousness of his or her opponents to keep them anxious and off-balance	"If you really cared about this family, you wouldn't complain about my needing to unwind on the weekends. You have no idea how hard I work—and all for you!"
Shaming	Using subtle sarcasm, ridicule, mocking, rolling eyes, and verbal put-downs to increase fear and self-doubt	"I wouldn't have to be rude to your mother if you could stand up for yourself with her."
Playing the Victim Role	Invoking pity in the listener so that he or she will excuse the other's bad behavior	"I only lied about seeing my ex because I knew how upset you would be. I only went to see him to get him to stop harassing us. You have no idea how hard that was for me!"
Vilifying the Victim	Making it appear as if he or she is responding to the provocation of someone else	"If you weren't such a complainer, I would have told you that the car had no gas in it. I just couldn't stand to hear you whine about it."
Playing the Servant Role	Cloaking a self-serving agenda in a noble cause	"My coworker begged me to help her move this weekend, so I won't be around to help with the kids. She really needs me."
Seducing	Charming, praising, flattering others to get them to lower their defenses and surrender their trust and loyalty	"You know you are my best girl, my favorite! You don't ever need to be jealous even if it looks like I am paying more attention to those other girls. They can't hold a candle to you."
Projecting Blame	Blaming others, shifting the blame to someone else	"Why did your mother have to tell you she saw me with someone else? What a blabbermouth she is. I am sick of her spying on me. She has no idea what she's talking about."
Feigning Innocence	Pretending to be unaware of what he or she is doing	"Your feelings got hurt? Really? I can't believe that. All I did was tell a little joke."
Feigning Ignorance or Confusion	Acting as if he or she doesn't know what the other person is talking about	"I have no idea what you are talking about. I barely even spoke to that other girl."

Brandishing Anger	Deliberately displaying anger to intimidate and coerce others; yelling, name-calling, swearing, being physically intimidating, towering over the other person	"If I have to listen to one more complaint from you, I am going to lose it!"
Distorting What the Other Person Is Saying or Doing	Purposefully obfuscating the issue by accusing the other person of saying or doing something he or she did not say or do	"How dare you accuse me of gambling!" (when the topic was why there isn't enough in the accounts to cover the expenses)
Withdrawing Love and Approval	Sulking, refusing to respond, becoming emotionally distant in order to induce fear of abandonment in the other person	"If that is what you think, then I don't know if we can be together."
Indicating Contempt for the Other Person	Mocking, ridiculing, rolling eyes, laughing, or otherwise showing that he or she has no respect for the other person's thoughts and feelings	"Stop being so nutsy."
Acting as the Final Authority, Defining Reality	Speaking in an authoritative manner, making unilateral decisions, discounting the other person's views	"The problem with you is . . ."
Criticizing in a Harsh and Uncalled-for Manner	Frequent and undeserved complaints and criticisms that undermine the person's sense of safety and security	"You are so pathetic with your little complaints. Why don't you just grow up?!"
Not Listening, Interrupting	Not allowing the person the freedom and respect to share their thoughts and feelings	"I have heard enough of your complaints."

Gottman can readily identify, based on the presence of these four horsemen, which marriages will ultimately fail.[14] The four horsemen as identified by Gottman are these: criticism, contempt, defensiveness, and stone-walling. They represent a distillation of the power and control techniques described above. When present to a high degree in a relationship, they represent a lack of love, respect, and emotional security. It is easy to imagine that a thin slice of any of the marriages depicted in this book would reveal most, if not all, of these horsemen of doomed marriages. It is really no surprise (in hindsight, admittedly) that these marriages failed.

Domestic Violence

Through using strategies of power and control and engaging in the four horsemen, the future alienator is able to maintain the upper hand in the relationship (as well as sow the seeds of marital failure). According to domestic violence expert Lundy Bancroft, in *Why Does He Do That? Inside the Minds of Angry and Controlling Men*, people who need to exercise their control over another person are engaging in abusive behavior.[15] Bancroft identifies abusers' central characteristics, many of which apply to the future targeted parent and future alienator relationship. Some have already been mentioned above—being controlling and manipulative, and denying and minimizing his/her behavior. Four psychological characteristics of perpetrators of domestic violence seem particularly salient for understanding the mindset of a future alienator. These are discussed below.

First, abusers experience a sense of entitlement, a right to treat others as he or she wants with no regard for others' rights or feelings. According to the dictionary, the term *entitlement* refers to a notion or belief that one is deserving of some particular reward or benefit. In the marriages described in the stories submitted for this book, the future alienators appeared to experience their needs as more real, their opinions as more worthy, and their viewpoints as more valid than the needs, opinions, or perspectives of their spouses. When Annette asked John whether he could understand that she had a separate opinion from his, his response was that she was either crazy or a liar. John was so convinced of the rightness of his opinions and experiences that anything else was to be wholly discounted.

If this sounds a lot like the definition of a narcissist, that's because it is. According to the American Psychiatric Association in the *Diagnostic and Statistical Manual of Mental Disorders*, fifth edition, one of the characteristics of a narcissistic personality disorder is "a sense of entitlement (i.e., unreasonable expectations of especially favorable treatment or automatic compliance with his or her expectations)."[16] This sense of entitlement was pervasive in the marriages described in the stories submitted and, as we shall see in the next chapter, pervasive in the unfolding alienation drama.

The fact that personality disorders such as narcissism, borderline, and antisocial provide a psychic platform for alienation has also been discussed by Baker in *Adult Children of Parental Alienation Syndrome: Breaking the Ties that Bind*. Specifically, Baker notes that the characteristics of the narcissist predispose such a person to disregard the feelings or needs of others and to feel justified in doing so. This paves the way for the alienation.

A second characteristic of abusers is their belief in their own superiority and their disrespect for the rights and feelings of others. Was Sean's wife thinking about Sean's desire to be near the center of action as his children were being born? Was Jack thinking about whether Marie would be tired the next day at work after staying up late typing his papers? Was John thinking about how Annette felt when he flirted with other women or shared hotel rooms with them? Was Tracy thinking about Marty's need for the truth about her marital status? It appears not. These future alienators shared an inability or unwillingness to accommodate the needs and feelings of the other person. They appeared to lack empathy for the felt experiences of others and were so certain that they were right in all matters that the other person's thoughts and feelings were no longer relevant. The pregnancy is terminated, the house is purchased, financial decisions are made, the plan to move is hatched—all with no discussion with the other person.

A third characteristic of the abuser is possessiveness. Several of the future targeted parents wrote about their spouses' wanting to control their time and attention, limiting their contact and communication with others, including coworkers, friends, and family members. This may have been partly motivated out of a desire to limit external influences so that the person didn't question what was going on in the relationship. But it also may have been motivated by difficulty in sharing the loved one with others.

The final characteristic of an abuser that is relevant for understanding the future alienator is their feeling justified when behaving badly, coupled with an inability to take responsibility for the harm that their actions have caused. A typical sentiment would be something like "I had to lie to my spouse, because he would get so upset and make such a big deal about it," or "I was doing what was best for the family when I told my wife she couldn't speak to her parents anymore. She didn't give me any choice." Once future alienators give themselves permission to deny the consequences of their actions and to disregard the feelings of their spouse, they have no internal constraints on their behavior. They have free rein to act as they please, regardless of the pain they are causing to their spouses.

THE FUTURE ALIENATOR AS A PARENT

The warning signs and red flags are not just indicators that the future targeted parents were married to selfish spouses who exploited, dominated, and manipulated them, but also indicators that their spouse would—whenever necessary—use their power and control strategies to turn their children against them.

Red Flags for Alienation

The entitlement that the future alienators felt to a greater share of the marital benefits (however that was defined in the marriage) is also a red flag that the person would feel entitled to the children's loyalty and allegiance following the divorce. This could include making decisions about the children, controlling the finances, and having more discretionary time. A person who perceives his or her own needs as more real, pressing, important, and worthy than anyone else's needs will be tempted to experience her or his desire to have a relationship with the children as greater than the other parent's needs—or even the needs of the children to have a relationship with both parents. It is hard to imagine alienation occurring without a sense of entitlement on the part of the alienating parent.

The alienator must be either unable to perceive the other parent as having any legitimate rights and claims on the marital assets or the children or willing to disregard those rights in an effort to win at all costs or punish the other parent. The alienator feels entitled to more rights and/or entitled to override the rights of the other parent. Even during the courtship, there were signs that the future alienators were not capable of acting in an empathic and considerate fashion toward their spouses. A selfish quality was apparent but overlooked by the future targeted parent, until it became impossible to ignore.

A second quality that was troubling in the marriage and laid the groundwork for the alienation is a sense of possessiveness that the future alienators expressed toward the future targeted parents and then transferred to the children. The future alienators viewed the future targeted parents more as objects to own and control than as separate, independent human beings with their own autonomous experiences. Likewise, the children were viewed as objects to own rather than as separate living beings who should, and can, be cared for by both parents. Owning the children and depriving the other parent of the opportunity and pleasure of parenting them appeared to be a driving force fueling the alienation.

Third, a belief in one's superiority can lay the groundwork for alienation because the future alienator can convince himself that the children will be better off with him or her. They will be convinced of the rightness of their opinions about childcare, the children's education, extracurricular activities, medical needs, and so forth, regardless of the fact that the other parent may have been as involved, if not more, in the raising of the children.

Fourth, devaluation of the other parent appears to also be a common thread throughout the stories. Some of the future alienators had experience cutting off people who displeased them. As one man wrote, "When I look back I see that she always saw the world as 'us versus them.'" A woman told how her husband of twelve years "refused to speak or see his mother. He also refused to talk to his sister because she came to our house unannounced one time." With experience and an apparent comfort with cutting people off, it is within their repertoire of acceptable behaviors to sever the children's relationship with their other parent. Their past method of operation appears to have been consistent with alienation.

The most obvious red flag of all, of course, however, is a prior history of alienating a child from their other parent in a previous relationship. At least one of the future alienators, Tracy, was already an alienator when Marty met her, and there cannot be a better predictor of her becoming an alienator in their relationship than already being one. In some of the other stories, the future alienator (or someone in his or her family) had alienation in their history. One man married a woman whose sister had cut her daughter off from the girl's father, while another man described how his girlfriend's daughter's father was "constantly belittled and made fun of. . . . It was a nonstop activity and was exacerbated whenever the father did show up," and one woman described how her husband made his daughter reject her mother and accept him as the better parent: "I was stunned to hear how vile he could be."

In sum, the relationships described in chapter 2 can be considered abusive in that the future alienator was not able to consistently or adequately respect the needs and feelings of the future targeted parent. The future alienators engaged in a range of power and control tactics that allowed them to override the needs of their spouse, the future targeted parent.

Despite the red flags that their future spouse would be a bad partner for them, and despite the red flags that their spouse would be a future alienator, these young, naïve, gullible, trusting future targeted parents still could not believe the world of pain and suffering that awaited them as they began the next phase of their lives as the former spouse of a future alienator.

Part II

Stolen Hearts, Stolen Minds

Chapter Four

Alienation in the Making

ANNA'S STORY

When did the alienation begin? In some ways it started the day we brought our child, Sonya, home from the hospital—when my husband, George, told me that I wasn't looking at our new daughter in the right way. There were also seeds of alienation in how he would tell our eighteen-month-old that I was a bad mommy.

He also bragged to me shortly after we divorced (when Sonya was about three and a half) that when Sonya asked to call me from his house he would ask her if it was because (a) I was making her call me or (b) she was worried about me. I, of course, was horrified and tried to explain that he was planting the seeds of doubt in her mind and that perhaps she was calling because she missed me. He couldn't seem to fathom this possibility. I felt so sad for my little girl who was being given the message that she was not allowed to miss her mommy. George also told me that he felt that I was preventing Sonya from calling him while she was home with me and that he had told her to make sure to not let Mommy do this. He failed to see the hypocrisy because, in my opinion, he failed to see anything from anyone else's own point of view but his own. This was the main reason I had left him, but I was still shocked (although I shouldn't have been) at his blatant efforts to interfere in my relationship with my daughter.

The alienation was present when Sonya was four years old and came home after a weekend with her father and accused me of stealing her college money. She certainly didn't know what college was and she barely knew what money was. What she did know was that I was doing something bad to her and her father was trying to protect her. She was angry and sobbing and screaming at me. This was one of the saddest things I had ever experienced, and so totally unnecessary. There was absolutely no truth to this claim (although he used actual events to create that appearance), but there was no way to explain this to a four-year-old. I tried my best to reassure her that I loved her and would never steal her money. I went to bed that night wondering how many assaults on our trust our relationship could withstand.

The alienation was in full force by the time Sonya's father remarried when Sonya was five years old. I recall one night, while putting Sonya to bed, when she explained to me that her stepmother, Margaret, was only nice to her if she called her "Mom." What could I say? I didn't want my daughter calling someone else "Mom," but I also wanted her stepmother to treat her with loving kindness.

Margaret had been married before and had children as well. What I would later learn is that George and Margaret began to take each of their respective ex-spouses to court on a regular basis to (a) increase the child support Margaret was to receive from her ex, while decreasing the child support George would pay to me—despite refusing to submit George's financial documents; and (b) increase George's parenting time by playing up the importance of fathers, while decreasing Margaret's ex-husband's parenting time. They had an aggressive attorney who was working double time, and in the course of about two years there were at least three hearings with me and as many, if not more, with Margaret's ex-husband. I began to dread the mail delivery, never knowing what new packet of lies and deception would be waiting for me.

I realized that there was virtually no relationship between what my ex claimed about me in court and reality. For example, he complained that I had taken my child to eight pediatricians rather than provide stable medical care, that I had taken her to a nude beach, and that I squandered her child support money. He seemed to follow the strategy that if he threw enough mud on the wall, something would stick, and because each time we went to court, he was rewarded with increased parenting time, he was right.

At one point he filed a motion against me and while in court I pointed out to the mediator we were sent to that George had booked a vacation out of the country with my daughter during my parenting time (despite having vacation time of his own) and without even telling me. Rather than reprimanding George for his behavior, the mediator shook his head in awe and proclaimed that he wished he had a father who cared as much about him.

I was learning that appearances mean a lot in court and George packaged his campaign against me in the guise of being a devoted father. I wish his devotion had been the case, but the truth was far less attractive. The reality was that George was a dominating father who demanded that his children (my daughter and his two stepsons) worship and admire him OR ELSE! People I know who were familiar with what was going on in George and Margaret's home spoke of how terrified the children were of crossing George. He was particularly strict and derisive with his youngest stepson, who, one year for Halloween, was wrapped in an old piece of carpet and presented as "a remnant."

Throughout these years I was continually told by my friends and family to stop obsessing about what George was doing because I was giving him too much power to make my life miserable. I was told to rest assured that my daughter knew which parent had her best interests at heart and that I could never lose her to her father because I was the primary parent. Lawyers I went to told me that there was nothing I could do because George wasn't physically abusing my daughter.

The alienation increased during Sonya's elementary school years despite our also having many loving moments together. I began to feel that my ex was my own personal terrorist. I never knew what trouble he would inflict on me and in what way he would intrude into my life. When Sonya was nine, I remarried and my new husband and I moved to a larger house. I heard from mutual acquaintances that Margaret was upset by this. This might explain the increase in tension between George and me.

George started to show up twenty minutes early every other Saturday morning for his parenting-time pick-up. One time I answered the door and calmly explained that Sonya wasn't ready, and she would come out at the appointed time. (I would have invited him in, but the last time I did that, he stole money from me.) His response was to yell at me that I should have called him if Sonya wasn't going to be ready early. He slammed the door in frustration and stormed away. When he came back at the right time I heard him berate Sonya, asking her, "Where were you? Why did you make me wait?" After that, Sonya insisted on being ready for her father at least twenty minutes before he was due to come just in case he came early. She also insisted on waiting outside for those twenty minutes even if it meant standing in the pouring rain or freezing cold. It seemed obvious to me that her father had impressed upon her the importance of not making him wait for her ever again, and she was willing to comply despite the inconvenience for her (or us).

Sonya also seemed to be under pressure to report to George about the workings of our home and finances and to keep secrets from us. In this way she was recruited into the campaign against us. No matter what I bought for her, she would call her father as soon as she could to tell him exactly what was purchased and how much it cost. I could sometimes hear him on the other end of the phone complaining about how cheap I was. Once I heard her respond back, "I know," despite my having just spent over two hundred dollars on a new wardrobe for her.

One time she revealed to a third party in front of me that her father was taking her on a vacation the entire following week (even though it was my parenting time and my family was coming from out of town to visit). She had evidently known for some time, but hadn't been allowed tell me. By the time I found out, there was nothing I could do other than call George and point out to him that he was violating the parenting order. He was unconcerned. This made sense, since he had never been reprimanded for doing so before.

It turned out that George would be returning during my weekend. I told him that I wouldn't object to his taking Sonya out of school this one time and that I would expect him to return her to me for my weekend. Despite the agreement, when the weekend rolled around he called to tell me that he wasn't sure he would return her to me. He said that since I had made a nasty comment about the testosterone levels of his stepsons, he didn't think I deserved to have my parenting time. My head was spinning. I had no idea what he was talking about. I had no thoughts, ideas, or opinions whatsoever about his stepsons (other than to sympathize with them) and, as far as I knew, had made no derogatory comments about them in any way—and certainly not about their "testosterone levels." I had no idea what that would even mean. George kept me on the phone for over half an hour toying with me, saying, "Should I let you have Sonya this weekend or not? Hmmmm, I just cannot decide." In the end he didn't return her to me, and my family missed another opportunity to spend time with her.

One Sunday Sonya called to tell me that she wouldn't be coming home the next day per the parenting plan. She said she had something important to do with her family and would come home the following day. Later that day her father drove her to my home to slip an envelope under my front door. She didn't let me know she had been to the house, not even to say hello. I only knew she had been there because of the envelope. It was addressed by her to

Mrs. Jones (my married name) rather than to "Mom." Inside was a letter about how I needed to respect her voice and how important it was for her to be heard and understood by me. This was not language that she would normally use and I strongly suspected that she had been put up to this by her father. I later found out that the reason she wanted to stay an extra day at her father's house was because her father and stepmother had a court date against the father of Sonya's stepbrothers and she—as the older sister—wanted (or was told to want) to stay home to support her brothers, who would be testifying in court against their father.

As Sonya matured she developed many talents and interests, notably horseback riding, art, and playing the violin. By the time she was in middle school I was spending nearly the entire monthly child support payments on her extracurricular activities and working hard to arrange her schedule. One of the sticking points was that George had made it clear that no lesson or activity was to occur on his time. This was sometimes problematic. For example, she was invited to participate in an elite Saturday morning riding group. Her father didn't bring her to one lesson that fell on his weekends even though I had offered to pay for all of the lessons. This had been his pattern all along. When she was younger and played soccer, he didn't bring her to one game that fell on his weekends despite showing up for every game on my weekends and insisting that Sonya stand with him during breaks and halftime. Likewise, he was present for every riding lesson or event that occurred on my time. Not only was he present, but he also monopolized Sonya's time and attention. He would even make nasty comments to her about me, complaining that he didn't like the way that I failed to greet him.

Sonya begged me to speak with him and so I began to approach him and say hello. Later Sonya told me that he didn't like the way I said hello. I would usually end up standing by while she ignored me and lavished all of her attention on her father, despite the event taking place during my parenting time and the fact that I was the one who arranged and supported her in her activities.

One weekend her riding stable had an all-day horse show that Sonya competed in. I paid all of the entry fees and brought her early in the morning, excited to watch her ride. When her father and his friends showed up, she acted as if I didn't exist. During the entire ten hours that we were all there together, she didn't say more than five words to me. When she wasn't riding, she stood next to her dad and watched the other events. He draped his arm around her in a possessive manner, smirking at me across the ring.

The alienation went into high gear in eighth grade, when Sonya revealed to me one night that her father wanted her to speak to a psychiatrist in order to say that she wanted to live with her father full-time. She presented it to me as something that she couldn't wait to do. She said it was only fair to Daddy. When I heard this, I worried that all was lost. I could imagine a time when I would have no relationship with my daughter at all. Shortly after that, Sonya's school held a concert. Excited to tape Sonya in all three performances—in the band, in the jazz band, and in the orchestra—I arrived with my video camera on the night of the school's musical concert. This was a first for the school and I was thrilled that Sonya was advancing in her musicianship. I saw the students take the stage and realized with a start that Sonya was not among them. I quickly gathered my things and went backstage to ask the teacher where Sonya was. I was informed that she had called to say that she was a bad girl and couldn't participate in the concert that night because the family was having a crisis. I was shocked (although, again, I shouldn't have been) that George would allow/force Sonya to let her classmates and teachers down and couldn't imagine the inconvenience that this would cause for everyone else, as she was the concert mistress and a soloist.

I raced home to tell my husband and he convinced me that we should go immediately to Sonya's therapist to tell her what was going on. When we arrived we found Sonya in the waiting room. George and Margaret were in with the therapist. After they left the office the therapist told us that Sonya told her father that she didn't actually want to change the living arrangements and that George and Margaret were furious that she had lied to them. The therapist said that she was astonished at Sonya's lying. I tried to explain to her that Sonya was under tremendous pressure to please her father and that she had virtually no choice but to lie. The therapist (who, it turned out, was a friend of a friend of George and Margaret) didn't see it that way.

Shortly after this event, George and Margaret went into crisis mode, claiming that Sonya was a pathological liar and a thief, saying she stole jewelry. (George later admitted to Sonya that Margaret had planted the jewelry under her bed.) George wrote Sonya a long letter explaining how valiantly he had tried to protect her from my mental illness, but she had failed to learn the appropriate lessons from him and Margaret, whom he described to Sonya as "your most ardent supporter, though you haven't got a clue." He said that he had lost all respect for her and that she was in danger of losing his love. He wrote, "The depth of your pathology astounds me."

At this point Sonya could do nothing right and she was no longer welcome in their home. One Sunday, to my great surprise and relief, George delivered Sonya to my house and sped away. She rang the bell and asked me if she could come in. (As if I would ever turn her away!) From that point on, her father refused to even speak with her. He had originally agreed to see her in therapy once a week, but he canceled the sessions, and it was clear that he had written her off. Her stepbrothers refused to speak to her as well—even though they went to the same school. A few weeks later, George and Margaret chaperoned the eighth-grade weekend school trip and they shunned Sonya the entire time. Not long after that I drove by George and Margaret's home and found all of Sonya's belongings on the curb. I wasn't surprised when I later saw a "For Sale" sign on the house, and shortly after that I heard that they had moved an hour away.

The next year was the best year ever for Sonya. She lost her extra weight, became a straight-A student, and excelled in riding, violin, and her latest sport, fencing. She was given a leading role in the high school musical—virtually unheard of for a freshman. Although I periodically worried that her father would come back for her, I naïvely believed that she would see how much happier and successful she was without him in her life to confuse and abuse her.

How wrong I was!

On May 29, nearly at the end of ninth grade, I arrived home from work one day to find Sonya sitting in the living room. "You will never guess who came to school today. You won't be happy, but I sure am!" she said with a big smile on her face.

My heart never sank so fast. I had heard a few weeks earlier that George and Margaret had broken up, and I feared that he would want to reengage with Sonya.

My worst fears were borne out, as he had shown up at her school with tears in his eyes, claiming that all of the bad things that had happened between them were due to that monster, Margaret. Sonya was desperate enough for her father's love that she believed this, despite its being utterly inconsistent with the facts. She was also disarmed by the fact that her father had shown his weakness to her, believing that this meant things would be different between them.

The heart wants what the heart wants. And my little girl's heart was not done wanting her father to be a good and loving father.

What proceeded was a long terrible tenth grade for Sonya as her relationship with her father slowly consumed her. Her grades fell, her weight went back up, and she fought with her teachers and coaches. Her father had fired her tutors and violin teacher. I tried to explain to Sonya that her father would only be happy if he cut her off from everyone and everything that mattered to her, but she didn't see it that way.

I once described it as watching a monster slowly eat my child alive. By the time tenth grade was over, the monster had consumed my child.

My child was gone, and our relationship was over.

JOE'S STORY

In the early years I spoke to my wife's ex-husband only one time. He told me, "She will do the same thing to you that she has done to me. She will take your kids and leave you with nothing." I rejected the idea, believing it was coming from a jaded loser. He wound up living on his mother's couch without much to brag about. Moreover, my wife, Kelly, had conditioned me to believe her ex-husband's situation was a result of his poor choices and not to feel sorry for him or see things from his point of view. I could never imagine that this man, for whom I had such little respect, would one day become an important witness for me in the custody case to win my children.

I have two kids—my son's name is Matt and my daughter is Eve. My children's minds were not kidnapped overnight by their mother; it took her many years to achieve that goal. Like a cult leader, my ex-wife masterfully chipped away at their ability to think for themselves or know their own truth. When it began, I had no idea of the fire being started right in front of me.

When my children were young, I worked a lot of hours to make ends meet. I would come home just in time for Kelly to leave and go to night school. She didn't like her job as a hairstylist, so she decided to go back to school and become an ultrasound technician. I would be with the kids while she was taking classes. One night in September I was able to come home early. When I walked into the kitchen, I read no happiness on Kelly's face. In its place was a look of shock that I was home so early. I scanned the room and noticed her haircutting equipment on the table along with a number of beer bottles. I questioned her about whose hair she had done that day and she told me it was one of the kid's friends, but she could not give me the name of the friend. When I asked who was drinking the beer, she had no answer to that either.

I took her phone off the counter and she feverishly tried to grab it from me. To my horror, I could see that there were numerous calls as well as explicit text messages from someone named Don. A spirited argument erupted and I demanded some answers. She didn't have any. In my frustration I broke her phone in half, something I have never been proud of. Close to me was a large rubber tree plant her mother had given her as a gift. In my frustration I snapped a branch off of that as well. But I never laid a finger on my wife. Kelly became hysterical, and she hollered for her son, from a previous marriage, to run to the neighbor's house and call 911. She scooped up our daughter and ran out of the house, yelling that I was beating her.

When the police arrived, they found Kelly sitting in the front yard cradling Eve in her arms. She told them a story about me threatening her. She explained that I had I thrown her on the ground with our daughter in her arms and tried to choke her. She also reported that I "trashed" the house and that she was now afraid for her life. This was all happening so quickly that I could not begin to process how my life was being destroyed.

All I could think of to do was to offer to escort the officers into the house to have a look around so that they could see for themselves that the house had not been "trashed." Before entering, they wanted to know if I had firearms in the house. Firearms! I didn't even own a BB gun. I assured the officers that the only thing they would find would be a broken cell phone and a broken branch of a plant. The police searched the house and discovered exactly what I said—a broken cell phone and a broken rubber tree plant. A female officer checked Kelly for bruises or scratches and found nothing. Thinking this nightmare was over, I learned I was still being asked to leave my property and that Kelly was requesting a restraining order. The officers gave me ten minutes to collect some belongings and they allowed me to drive my own car behind them to the station. I never returned to my home again.

Needless to say, I was feeling quite angry and hurt and, above all else, confused. I thought of the warning her first husband had given me and could not believe that his prediction was coming true. I was a broken man sleeping in my car. I learned that in cases of domestic violence, a man is usually guilty until proven innocent. I also learned that in order to prove my innocence, I would need time and a lot of money, neither of which I had.

A few weeks after I was removed from my house, I had heard from a neighbor that Kelly moved a new man into our home. I was beginning to understand just how deep the deception was. A year earlier she had asked if she could help me out with the finances. She said she was making the offer to assist me because I worked so much and she hated to see me having to deal with all the bills as well. She would eventually become our bookkeeper.

Fearful, I began to make phone calls to our credit card company and the bank that held both our mortgage and our car loan. My legs became wobbly when I learned that she had been paying nothing to any of them! Moreover, the credit card had outrageous bills to restaurants, hotels, and day spas. The house was about to go into foreclosure and the car was due to be repossessed. I had to ask myself, "Who was this woman I had been living with all these years?"

As I made another phone call to the college she was attending, I wondered if my capacity for shock would ever run out. The nice lady in the admissions department told me that Kelly was not a student there. Evidently, she had been keeping the tuition money I had given her, along with the money for the mortgage and car payments. I learned that during the times when she told me she was in school, she was actually in a local bar looking for her next boyfriend. Her actions would eventually force me into bankruptcy.

I learned that her plan was to put the house into foreclosure and have her new boyfriend, Nick, sweep in and buy it at a significant discount. Luckily, I was able to prevent that from happening by selling the house in a short sale and walking away with half of what it was worth. A few months later her car was also repossessed, which resulted in my kids being without a home or a car, something she would gladly blame on me. "What kind of monster would take away his children's house and car and leave them with nothing?" she would announce to everyone. To solve her problem, she and Nick moved the kids to an apartment in a different town. Nick became her new savior and my replacement.

Soon it became her word against mine. She approached my closest confidants and told them horrible stories of abuse and mistreatment. The children would spend the next few years hearing about how Daddy beat Mommy and was removed from the house in handcuffs. In the beginning I couldn't afford to fight the false allegations in court. I had just filed for bankruptcy, my lawyer's bills were more than I made in a month, and I was living in my car. My life was hopelessly tangled and all I wanted was my children. I did have court visitation rights but couldn't let them see how I was living, so I couldn't take them for full weekends because I had no place for the kids to sleep. Sometimes I would drive into their town, call their mother, and beg to take them out for ice cream or to a movie, and she would withhold them from me. She knew I didn't have the money to take her back to court. I would work overtime to try to dig myself out of this hole, and she would take me back to court for an increase in child support due to the extra money I was making. I was working harder and longer and it was all going to her. I was trapped.

When I was younger, I lost my brother in a horrible accident. That experience made me realize the importance of family and I was determined to not lose my own flesh and blood to my ex-wife. I launched into the fight of my life. I surrounded myself with positive people and slept on many of their couches to save money. Their homes became places I could bring my children and spend time with them. Although it wasn't ideal, I was able to see my children.

On the weeks I didn't see them I would call and ask to speak with them. I was never able to. I was told they were, "playing with the cat" or didn't want to talk to me. Once I phoned and my ex-wife and her friends kept the receiver off the hook with me on the other end of the line so that I could hear. They said things like "How long do you think this idiot will stay on the phone?" and "What a loser! Doesn't he know his kids can't stand him?" My kids were in the room at the time and could surely hear what was being said about me.

My name in town would be forever tarnished by Kelly's false accusations. I tried to stay up-to-date with the kid's grades and activities, but when I attended school conferences the expression of pure hatred crossed the faces of the teachers as they looked at me. I couldn't fault them, as they were being fed lies about my being a criminal and an abusive father.

Sometimes during my parenting time, my children would ask me about the terrible things they were hearing about me. My daughter would ask me questions about why I used to choke Mommy. My son wondered why I hadn't gone to his graduation from middle school, when his mother had never told me about it. The poison she fed them about me was endless and it broke my heart to think that my children would even wonder whether I could do these things.

I had finally scraped up enough money to start over and I bought a home in a different town. Word of my getting my life back together put Kelly in pure misery and she devised another trick for me. The court agreement for the kids' health care was for me to pay 80 percent of the bill, and Kelly 20 percent. She figured out how to rack up bills and make me waste money by taking the kids to the emergency room even when they weren't really sick. This happened on a monthly basis. I started receiving bills for $2,000 because my son had a cold and bills for X-rays performed on the children for every bump or bruise. Eventually the insurance company stopped paying altogether. When I questioned this practice, I was again accused of not having the children's best interests at heart and being cheap and cruel.

Despite this campaign against me, I was inspired that the children still wanted to spend time at my house. As Kelly realized that her efforts were not working as quickly as she had hoped, she stepped it up a notch. She began to make every one of my custodial weekends a celebration at her house so that the kids would be reluctant to leave her to come be with me. She would arrange playdates and sleepover parties on my time, as well as trips to water parks and fairs. It became a ritual each Thursday night to get a call from one of my kids to ask me if they could stay home that weekend so as not to miss out on what their mother had planned. I put my foot down once or twice and learned not to do that again, since the kids resented me for it and spent the entire weekend sulking because their mother carried on with the excitement without them.

The day Kelly had been working for finally came one Thursday in the spring. Matt was set up to phone me and ask if he could attend a bonfire that Friday on my time. He said, "It's okay with Mom." Although aggravated, I entertained the idea in order to not upset my son. I asked the normal fatherly questions such as "Whose house was the bonfire going to be at? Until what time?" and "Will the parents be home?" Matt did not know the answers to any of these questions. I asked him to please put his mother on the phone.

I could hear her grumble in the background that she would not talk to me. Highly irritated, I explained that unless I had these answers, I could not allow him to go to his bonfire. Without incident my son said, "Okay," and hung up the phone. A moment later I received a text message from Kelly saying, "Nice job dad, now your son is crying. What kind of abusive bastard are you?" I phoned Matt back and he told me he never wanted to see me again.

I did not see my son again for eighteen months.

NORA'S STORY

It has been eight years since I last saw or heard from my two sons. It is as unbelievable to me today as it was when I first lost them. Both of my sons were alienated from me at the same time—my older son was then sixteen years old and my younger son was thirteen. There is not a day that I don't think about them and have a lump in my throat.

When my older son Brad was two years old, I realized that there were some peculiarities in his development and behavior. He wasn't keeping up with the other children he played with; he wasn't saying "bye-bye," playing peek-a-boo, or learning language the way the other kids were. Something just didn't feel right. I couldn't pinpoint what it was, but I felt that this fear was more than about just being a first-time mom. At that time I was pregnant with my second son, Arthur. When I was five months pregnant I was told that the amniocentesis revealed an abnormality in his DNA structure: he might have mental retardation, blindness, or some other disability that couldn't be identified. I was five months pregnant, had grave doubts about the development of my then older son, and was given a window of three weeks to decide whether to terminate the pregnancy due to fetal abnormalities. It was the hardest decision of my life.

Of course, I turned to my husband so that we could make this decision together. I shared with him my feelings about Brad and asked what he thought we should do about my pregnancy. I will never forget what he said or how it made me feel. His response to me was "No mother who says there is something wrong with her son could ever be a good mother." And, "If you cannot take care of one child, why would you think you could take care of another?" He also said that while he didn't have an opinion about abortion, it should be my decision alone to have the baby, since I was the mother and would be the one raising him. Something froze inside me in that moment. I realized that I was not married to a loving spouse; I was married to a cold person who did not really care about me or our family. I was devastated. When I needed his loving compassion the most, he was not there for me.

I shouldn't have been surprised by his callousness because all along what impressed me most about Scott was his cool intellect; he had never been particularly warm. Since he was an Ivy League graduate and I only had an associate's degree, I looked up to him and relied on his intelligence. I assumed that he was smarter than me. However, as I was finding out, what he had in intelligence, he severely lacked in compassion, love, and the ability to connect with others.

As an example of his coldness, for twelve years he refused to speak to or see his mother. He said she had a negative personality. He also refused to talk to his sister because she came to our house unannounced one time. He was equally harsh with my own family. When my mother and father wanted to come across the county to visit, Scott would not let them spend the night at our house. He insisted that they stay in a hotel, and even then they were allowed to spend no more than one week in town. He counted the days until they were gone. Over the sixteen years of our marriage he explained his many rules to me with complete certainty in their rightness and logic. He explained that if you let people stay longer, they may stay forever. Listening to him, I thought he seemed so rational, so smart. I didn't have the confidence in myself to argue.

I thought long and hard about my pregnancy. Ultimately I decided to have this child, my son, regardless of the outcome. I knew that I loved him. I had no way of knowing until he was born what his disabilities would be. Only time would only tell. I thought of him as my Mother's Day gift because he was born the Friday before the holiday. I chose his name because it was a favorite name of his father's and I wanted to make sure his father would love him.

So here I was—a young mother with two sons, many concerns, and a husband who seemed to be more and more heartless to me. He had so many rules for me to follow. For example, because he worked all day talking to people, he insisted that all of the phones be turned off at night. He also had a rule about my not being able to walk past the boys' bedroom when they were asleep so that I would not wake them up. He said I brushed their hair in the wrong direction, I brushed their teeth too hard, and I trimmed their nails too short. We were not allowed to wear open-toe shoes/sandals. Keeping track of these rules exhausted me mentally and physically.

When Arthur was nine months old and Brad started preschool, my fears for my older son grew, while my concerns for my younger son abated. When the preschool teacher asked to have an appointment with me, I knew it would not be good. She said although she and the other teachers could fill a book with everything wonderful about Brad, they wouldn't be doing their jobs if they didn't tell me their concerns. They said that I needed to take him for a neurological evaluation and have him tested. We went to UCLA and it was confirmed that my son, my wonderful, beautiful, sweet son, was diagnosed with autism. I felt a range of emotions—disbelief, devastation, sadness, anger, validation, and a bit of relief, because now that I knew the diagnosis I could get to the task at hand, which was caring for my son and doing whatever it would take to get him the best possible life. Armed with the diagnosis, I focused on doing what I could for my son.

I was a stay-at-home mom; my husband worked as an attorney. I felt so grateful that I could stay home with my children. I would do anything and everything for them. My job was taking care of the home and family and my husband's job was his work. I believed this was a fair balance, so I—without hesitation—took it upon myself to learn as much as I could about autism. Even with everything that has happened, I can honestly say that I believe that my son has benefited from my involvement and support. I am very proud that my son learned how to have friends, that he has found acceptance among his peers, and that he went to a typical school with typical children. I would do anything for my children. And while I had the chance, I did as much as I could.

In contrast, Scott barely participated. He didn't attend teacher meetings, birthday parties, or social events with other parents. If we were invited anywhere, he would make an excuse not to go. Or, if he did go, he made it clear he was doing so under duress. Eventually it became easier for me to not even ask him and I would attend meetings and gatherings without him. I felt like a single mother.

So now, when I haven't seen my children for eight years, it is beyond astounding to me that their father, who never taught them to swim or to ride a bike, never went with them to Boy Scouts, hadn't participated in their lives, has brainwashed them against me.

It all happened after we got a divorce. I believed that even though you divorce a spouse, you do not divorce your children, and that all children need a dad, especially those with special needs—they need all the love they can get. So I tried to have an amicable divorce. Scott met a woman and after three months he became engaged, moved in with her, and moved the boys in with them. Although I wasn't pleased with this, I didn't try to stop it. One benefit to the new living arrangements was that it gave me more time with my sons. Scott asked if I could take the boys for three weeks out of a month instead of two. That was more than fine with me!

Even spending one week with their father seemed to be too much for them. One week, after being with his father, my son Arthur (who at this time was developing typically, no disability except for the chromosome abnormality) came back to me exhausted, depressed, and worried because he did not have his homework done for the next day. I asked him what was going on and he told me that his father said he was not there to help him with his homework, and that Arthur was old enough to do it on his own. And my son told me that his father had locked himself inside the bedroom, leaving both Arthur and his brother to fend for themselves. I vividly recall that night, reading aloud to my son the whole book he was supposed to read and doing all of the homework together.

Arthur also came home after one week with his father and told me that he had opened the bedroom door and seen his father and this woman together. That was extremely disturbing for me to hear and I couldn't even imagine how disturbing it was to my son. After two months, the woman broke off the engagement. I think perhaps she realized in just a few months what took me sixteen years to realize: that Scott was not a particularly caring person. At first I was hopeful that the situation would improve, but that was not to be. Scott insisted on reverting back to the original parenting plan, with one week on with the boys and one week off. It was hard for me (and I think it was hard for them) to spend so much less time together than we had been used to. We tried to adjust. At one point Scott sued me for full custody. He lost. But the stress was becoming too much for Brad and Arthur.

Something was changing in our relationship as my sons became more aligned with their father against me. When they would come back to me for my week, they would come to me as different people from when they left. They came back to my house rude and nasty toward me. They demanded that their father come into the house to adjust the thermostat, since he thought I kept the house too warm. When I protested, telling them their father was not to come in the house, they demanded to see the divorce agreement showing where it said he couldn't come in. They decided that I was no longer capable of helping them with their homework because their father went to a better university than I had. My sons were ten and thirteen years old at the time! And after all, they would exclaim, didn't I know that all women were illogical? They sounded more and more like their father and started refusing to come to me at all.

Heartbroken and searching for solutions and answers, I went to my attorney, a psychologist, another attorney specializing in divorces, and anyone who I thought might be able to assist me. Over and over I was told that, because of their ages, the boys could make their own decisions. My response then and now is that I do believe children can make their own decisions, but I believe these children weren't making their own decisions—that they were being brainwashed. And I believe that to brainwash a child with special needs should be a criminal offense. My ex should be charged with manipulating someone who should be protected by law. But to this day Scott continues to go unpunished for what he was done.

At one point a family specialist was assigned to our case. I have never felt more betrayed or outraged in my life. The family specialist was someone I knew and to whom I had taken my son for therapy. When I went to discuss the alienation with her, she told me that I was in denial about my relationship with the boys, that I was seeing our relationship through rose-colored glasses. She explained that my sons told her they had never been happy with me. My older son told her I had never accepted his autism and that I abused them. When I heard this I was speechless. She told me the boys could and should make their own decisions about spending time with me. The more I objected, the less sympathetic toward me she became.

This was true of others as well. The more I tried to tell my side of the story, the more everyone disbelieved me. My family, some friends, and one of my son's teacher witnessed what I had gone through as a mother. That helped me to feel understood. Eventually I stopped feeling the need to explain myself. I stopped trying to get specialists to believe me. I no longer tried to explain what "parental alienation" means. Some people don't know, don't care, and don't care to know. I know the truth and that is what sustains me.

For the past ten years I have worked in the field of developmental disabilities. My goal is to make life better for individuals with developmental disabilities and for their families. I give advice and pass on to them what I feel has helped me, and I guide them through the process of receiving services and social programs. Some days it is really hard for me. I miss my sons with every ounce of my being. I miss the children that they once were. I feel I was robbed of their childhood and robbed of my motherhood. Birthdays and Mother's Day are especially hard for me. Sometimes when I am in the supermarket or out and about, I see a child who resembles one of my sons and my throat just about closes, the tears are always right behind my eyes.

There were a couple of times when I saw their father in the community and I approached him and asked him why he wouldn't let me see my children. He calmly said that I could see them anytime, that I could call them anytime. I have called, written e-mails, sent letters, sent gifts, and haven't yet received a response. I also must add that I am not the only one who has been alienated from Brad and Arthur. Their grandparents (my parents), aunt, uncle, and aunt on their father's side have also not been able to communicate or see them. Ironically, Scott's mother, whom he refused to speak to or see for twelve years, is back in his life. Sometimes I wonder if he will make me serve a twelve-year sentence like her.

Chapter Five

The Alienation Tipping Point

Each of the stories in chapter 4 is a heart-wrenching account of a parent waging a losing battle in the fight against alienation. Try as they might, the targeted parents were no match for the alienating parents' determined efforts to steal their children away from them. This chapter discusses the themes of alienation that are common across these stories.

PARENTAL ALIENATION STRATEGIES

The alienating parents were described as engaging in the very behaviors that research has found to be indicators of parental alienation. Not surprisingly, belittling of the other parent (by badmouthing them to the children) was nearly ubiquitous and was typically combined with a mix of other parental alienation strategies. Each story described at least half a dozen strategies that worked together to bind the child to the alienating parent, while creating a psychological wedge between the child and the targeted parent. Several points about the parental alienation strategies deserve special attention and discussion.

The first is the role of false allegations of physical and sexual abuse. This was mentioned in most of the stories and seems to serve at least three distinct functions. First, the accusation itself causes a harmful disruption of the relationship because the accused parent is legally prohibited from having contact with the children while the abuse investigation is being conducted. This provides the alienator with uninterrupted access to the children during which time he or she can hammer home the alienation message unfettered. In addition, there are fewer triggers for the child's positive memories with the targeted parent and no opportunity for the targeted parent to provide a corrective experience and remind the child that he or she really does love and cherish the child. Without the targeted parent to counter the negative messages the child is receiving, the child may be even more susceptible to believing them. The seeds of doubt and fear—left unchallenged—are more likely to take hold within the child.

The abuse accusation and subsequent investigation also are typically extremely stressful, if not traumatic, experiences for the accused parent and create a significant drain on that parent's financial and emotional resources. The targeted parent may make concessions in the custody case or may give up altogether in response to the stress and fear aroused by the investigation.

To the extent that a custody dispute can be viewed as a war, the false allegation is a very effective battle maneuver. In some states, knowingly making a false allegation is a criminal offense and a factor in the "best interest of the child" statutes. Practically speaking, however, alienating parents are rarely reprimanded, let alone penalized, for making a false allegation.

The allegation also serves to reinforce for the children that the alienating parent must be right because the courts, child protection, police, and so forth, appear to side with that parent. Children are generally too naïve and unsophisticated to appreciate that the child protection system is biased (as it should be) toward protecting children and, therefore, can easily be misused by devious and dishonest individuals seeking to gain the upper hand. In the mind of the child, "Mommy must be guilty because Mommy is not allowed to see me. She must have done something bad, just like Daddy said." In this way, simply the act of making the accusation creates the appearance of guilt in the eyes of the child.

That is why to a large extent it doesn't really matter what the result of the investigation is, because the process of being investigated creates the appearance of guilt—not just in the eyes of the children but also throughout the community. And if the finding does not support the allegation, the alienating parent can always claim that the system is corrupt or that the targeted parent was too clever to get caught. If these claims are made with sufficient earnestness, there is usually someone willing to believe them and assume that the targeted parent is guilty—even after being exonerated. Furthermore, many child protection investigations are resolved with the status of "insufficient evidence," a finding that can cast a shadow of doubt over a targeted parent's reputation for years to come.

Sometimes the false allegations are made to the police or child protection services, and sometimes to other authority figures (doctors, nurses, teachers, and coaches). Again, it is not the official finding that is meaningful, but rather the impression of danger created in the eyes of the children. One father wrote of a particularly harrowing experience he had on the day he went to the hospital to say goodbye to his dying father: "As I approached my father's hospital room, my (then) wife was peering out of his door. When she saw me coming, she grabbed my youngest son by the arm and ran to the nurse's station, claiming that I was violent and she and my son needed a safe way to exit. My eldest son remained in the room. Within a couple of minutes, hospital security came to the room, escorted me to an interview room, and threatened to call the police and have me arrested for assault." Reinforcing the idea that Dad must be dangerous, this vivid and dramatic experience was probably etched into the mind of the young boy who was escorted out of the hospital by the concerned nurses and the older son who remained to witness his father's interaction with security.

In addition to allegations of abuse, the content of ongoing badmouthing messages directed to the children appears to be designed to foster the belief that the targeted parent does not love them. Sometimes this is accomplished with innuendo and sometimes with outright statements, but the children appear to absorb the message regardless. One father who was consistently blocked in his efforts to spend time with his daughter later learned that she had been told, "Your dad doesn't want to see you anymore." It can sometimes be surprising to a targeted parent to understand that their child feels rejected by them because they experience themselves as the rejected party in this family drama. But, in reality, alienated children typically feel rejected by the very parent whom they are rejecting. Counterintuitive as this may be, it is very important to understand this, as it can help reinforce empathy for alienated children and suggest avenues for reconciliation later.

Some alienating parents quite ingeniously create the appearance that the targeted parents are rejecting their children when in fact those parents are working hard to maintain contact and preserve the relationship. A chilling example is when one man's ex-wife, with their daughter by her side, exclaimed "She *is* a good girl!" while on the phone with him. With only the mother's side of the conversation audible, the child couldn't tell that her father was not making disparaging comments about her. All she heard was her mother defending her. It is the rare child indeed who would be savvy enough to detect this lie.

THE ALIENATION TIPPING POINT

Many of the stories involved a protracted period of moderate alienation with the targeted parents living in a constant state of fear, knowing that, as bad as things were, they could always get worse. Anna wrote, "I went to bed that night wondering how many more assaults on our trust our relationship could withstand." In these families, the alienation ultimately did progress to the outcome most targeted parents feared: becoming completely cut off by their children.

This raises the intriguing question of what eventually tipped the children over to the other side. What precipitated the progression from moderate to severe alienation? In his exploration of tipping points In the fascinating book *The Tipping Point*, journalist Malcolm Gladwell highlights features of the messenger, the message, and the context within which the message is heard that help to create an unstoppable force.[1] Some of these features are particularly relevant to alienation.

First is the "stickiness" of the message. Gladwell points out that we are bombarded with thousands of messages every day (Internet advertising, bulletin boards, and so forth), but only a few are "sticky" enough to stay with us. Evidently, there are ways to package information to make it more or less irresistible, and sometimes small tweaks to the message can have a big impact on its effectiveness. This tweaking is what marketers do when they field-test new campaigns to craft the most compelling message.

Alienating parents also may "field test" their message to find the one that will stick with their children. Perhaps the most compelling message is that the other parent is crazy or a monster or has rejected the child. Alienating parents can try out these different messages until they find the one that takes hold inside the child. Most likely it will be the one that resonates with the child's own experiences of the targeted parent. For example, the alienating parent can take an actual event or quality of the targeted parent and reinterpret it for the child as evidence of that parent's rejection.

Gladwell also points out that children are hardwired to receive information that is presented in a narrative format (with characters and a plot that has a beginning, middle, and end). Narratives help children integrate disparate events, actions, and feelings into a single structure, a coherent whole that helps them make sense of the world. Once the outline of the story has been established, new information is incorporated in a way that is consistent with the original narrative. If the alienating parent is able to package the alienation as a "story" in which he is the hero, the child is the victim, and the other parent is the villain, the child will be primed to see unfolding events according to that storyline.

The targeted parent will have a hard time counteracting the negative message once it is internalized as the child's story of his family. Think, for example, of how Anna's husband told their daughter from an early age that "Mommy is a bad Mommy." In this way, he was creating a story about their family and providing a framework for how Sonya should feel about each of her parents.

Once the storyline is set, it is very hard to assimilate contradictory information. This is because the "deep need to repress inner contradictions is a fundamental property of the human mind," science reporter Jonah Lehrer observes in *How We Decide*.[2] Stories, according to science reporter David DiSalvo in *What Makes Your Brain Happy and Why You Should Do the Opposite*, make our brains "happy."[3] Once children are certain of the story, they stop listening to the part of their brain that says it might be wrong. A schemata of the family becomes embedded in the child's mind and information that does not fit that schemata is selectively ignored and actively rejected. This is because, as psychologists Carol Tavris and Elliot Aronson write in *Mistakes Were Made (But Not by Me)*, unfortunately, "most people when directly confronted by evidence that they are wrong, do not change their point of view or course of action but justify it even more tenaciously."[4] DiSalvo explains that neuroscience has uncovered the basis of this stubbornness by revealing that "[t]he state of being uncertain is an extremely uncomfortable place for our brains to live: The greater the uncertainty, the worse the discomfort."[5] In this way, the negative message the alienating parent wants the child to absorb about the targeted parent "sticks" in their brain.

Even a sticky message needs an effective delivery system. Gladwell refers to this as "the salesman." The alienating parent becomes a salesman who is particularly good at the art of persuasion, having a powerful sense of how to make their message irresistible. This trait "makes people who meet him want to agree with him" no matter what comes out of his mouth.[6]

In chapter 3, the future targeted parents described the future alienators as charming, captivating, and commanding. They were charismatic leaders who were able to sweep the future targeted parents off their feet, make them feel

safe and loved, and—at least for a while—persuade and coerce them into
obedience and subservience. The very qualities that sold the future targeted
parents on the original relationships were also put to use in selling the alienating messages to the children.

As important as the sticky message is, the effectiveness of the messenger
is even more so. According to classic social persuasion theory, the qualities
of the speaker account for the vast majority of the message conveyed to the
listener. Communication theory experts Winston Brembeck and William
Howell cite Emerson when they teach, "What you are speaks so loudly I
cannot hear what you say."[7]

The selling of ideas and products is a total mind and body experience. The
message is not just communicated through words. Gladwell summarizes the
research evidence indicating that how people respond to a communication is
greatly affected by perceptions about the communicator's intentions, expert-
ness, and trustworthiness.[8] The listener's interpretation of the knowledge and
character of the speaker determines, to a large extent, whether the content of
the message is absorbed. In this regard, the alienating parent has a distinct
advantage, being an actual parent and authority figure to the child. As more
than one formerly alienated child has proclaimed about their alienating parent, "Of course I believed that parent. To me she was God!"

The sticky alienation message is also conveyed nonverbally through body
language, emotions, and feelings. This is the kind of communication that the
alienating parents were probably particularly good at. Through the force of
their personality, they knew how to make their ideas compelling to the children—so compelling that it overrode their actual experiences. Gladwell
writes that "part of what it means to have a powerful or persuasive personality, then, is that you can draw others into your own rhythms and dictate the
terms of the interaction."[9] He notes that even when we are aware of these
qualities—and children generally are not—we may find the effective salesman hard to resist. The alienating parents crafted their sticky message so that
it would seem like the targeted parent didn't love the child. They sold it to
the children through the effectiveness of their persuasion.

Persuasion works in subtle ways we cannot always appreciate. Psychologist and influence expert Robert Levine reports that most people have the
illusion that they are immune to persuasion.[10] For example, they think that
advertising works on others, but not on them. Therefore, children who are in
the process of being alienated are most likely unaware of what is happening
to them. It might have even been hard for the targeted parents themselves to

identify how the alienators were doing it, as persuasion tactics are usually (although not always) subtle, hidden, and unspoken. However, even if the targeted parents could have put their finger on it and explained it step by step to their children, they would have been met with anger and indignation.

The art of persuasion is so compelling that the person experiences the implanted idea as authentic rather than as forced upon them from an external force. Consider, for example, research that shows that people instructed to nod their head up and down while listening to a message are more likely to endorse the message than people instructed to shake their head side to side. [11] The research subjects were entirely unaware of the impact of the head movement on their beliefs and experienced their agreement with the message as based on a rational appraisal of the merits of the argument. Likewise, a child instructed by an alienating parent to "show me that you are listening to me and understand that I am telling you that your father doesn't love us anymore" may nod his or her head in agreement and hence, unaware of the tactics used to gain her or his allegiance, be inclined to agree with that parent's message.

THE SIX TACTICS OF PERSUASION

Decades of psychological research and consumer marketing studies have identified the essential elements of the art of influence. What we know is that humans have evolved to make use of mental shortcuts to help navigate complex decision-making situations and social interactions. Because these shortcuts are not conscious, they can be activated outside of a person's awareness, through the use of persuasion tactics. When an alienating parent engages in one of more of these tactics, the child can be manipulated into believing the truthfulness of the alienation message the same way that consumers can be tricked into buying a product they don't need or want. In *Influence: The Psychology of Persuasion*, psychologist and persuasion expert Dr. Robert Cialdini describes six tactics, all of which can easily be applied to understand parental alienation. [12]

The first is the rule of reciprocity, which dictates that a person will generally feel obligated to reciprocate when given a gift or favor. A common employment of this rule is the marketing ploy of sending free gifts in the mail along with requests for donations. The recipient will unconsciously feel obligated to return the favor by making a donation, which he or she might not have made otherwise. All parents give things to their children, so the alienating parent has many opportunities to invoke this rule of reciprocity. That parent can do this, for example, by reminding the child of everything he or she has done for the child and signaling that something is expected in return (loyalty, preference, rejection of the other parent). The child's sense of indebtedness can be increased if the alienating parent creates the appearance of "going to battle" for the child, by claiming, for example, to be protecting the child, advocating for the child, or standing up for the child, or to have made sacrifices for the child. These are common themes in the stories of alienation throughout this book. For example, Sonya was led to believe that her father was trying to protect her from her mother's theft of her college funds.

The rule of reciprocity may also explain why alienated children are pressured to refuse gifts from the extended family of the targeted parent, as that would create an indebtedness toward *them*, something the alienating parent does not want to see happen. The child may also decline gifts to avoid feeling indebted to the targeted parent.

Second is the rule of consistency and commitment. As Cialdini explains, "Once we have made a choice or taken a stand we will encounter personal and interpersonal pressure to behave consistently with that commitment."[13] If the alienating parent can create a situation in which the child will betray the targeted parent (be rude, lie to, spy on, reject, and the like), the child will come to believe that the targeted parent must be unworthy. (Why else would the child have behaved the way he did?) The very act of betrayal creates inside the child an identity as someone who doesn't love or care for the other parent. If the child puts the betrayal in writing, this can further enhance the negative feelings, as people tend to believe that they mean what they write. This explains the frequency of alienated children being encouraged to write letters of rejection to their targeted parent. Think of Sonya's letter to her mother that was addressed to "Mrs. Jones" rather than "dear Mom." According to Cialdini, "Commitments are most effective in changing a person's self image and future behavior when they are active, public, and effortful."[14]

The commitment also must be perceived to be the result of free will. The external pressure must not be detectable. This, of course, fits well with the independent thinker phenomenon seen so frequently in alienated children who go out of their way to deny any external influence on their thoughts and feelings about the targeted parent.

Another aspect of commitment is that it should be incremental. It is unlikely that an alienating parent, after one negative statement, could convince a child to reject the other parent. But the parent can achieve that desired outcome by asking the child in small incremental steps to move in that direction. If the alienating parent can convince the child to make a small act of betrayal or unkindness to start with, it is more likely that the child will engage in a larger act of betrayal or unkindness later. Each step solidifies the child's commitment and moves that child in the desired direction. As with all of these tactics, the child must be unaware of the role of the alienating parent. The child must be convinced that he or she is willingly making his or her own choices at each step.

The endorsement of the social group is the third source of influence. People naturally look to others to understand how to behave, especially in a novel or uncertain situation. When uncertain, the reactions and behaviors of others can serve as a useful guide. Children are, of course, uncertain in many situations, as their life experience is so limited. When trying to make sense of their parents' divorce—a situation fraught with uncertainty—the views and perceptions of those in their social network will be especially salient for them. To the extent that the alienating parent has activated the social group to rally behind them (through the vilification of the targeted parent) and endorse their alienation message, the child will be likely to find the necessary cues for how to behave (i.e., believe that parent). This rule may also explain why younger children become alienated following the alienation of their older brother or sister; they are following the cues of their relevant social group.

The fourth weapon of social influence is likability. Generally speaking, the more likable someone is, the more they will successfully sell their product or message. Salient elements of likability are physical attractiveness, similarity, and flattery. It is easy to imagine that the alienating parents were high on the likability scale based on the descriptions of them provided in chapter 2. They were noted for their good looks, humor, warmth, and their ability to project kindness, success, and competence. Their winning personalities had swept the future targeted parents off their feet. The very features that made them so compelling as future mates also made them effective alienators.

One aspect of likability that may be particularly relevant for alienation is similarity. The more similar the child feels to the alienating parent, the more likable the parent will be to the child. If the alienating parent is able to enhance the child's sense of being more like that parent than the targeted parent, the stronger their alliance will be. For this reason, the alienating parent may accentuate their common physical features, sensibilities, tastes, skills, or talents.

Another way to enhance similarity is to create the feeling of being on the same team, working toward the same goals. Having a shared name that excludes the targeted parent seems to be a common ploy to create an "us vs. them" mentality. Alienating parents do this by acting as if they are protecting or speaking for the child. Once the children feel cohesion with that parent, they are probably more inclined to follow that parent's wishes. The alienating parent may have also been able to induce in the children a feeling of *not* liking the targeted parent. To the extent that the alienating parent creates rancor and disharmony between the child and the targeted parent (think of their difficulty setting limits or exercising parental authority), the child—by contrast—may come to feel that the alienating parent is that much more likable. In one story, the mother noted that even while married, her husband referred to her as "Crabby Mommy" and "The Big Bad Witch" when speaking to their children.

The fifth feature of influence is authority. Research has consistently demonstrated that individuals are highly susceptible to the dictates of authority figures. Of course, parents are actual authority figures for children. In theory, the two parents within a family should have equal degrees of authority over a child, and yet, in families affected by parental alienation, the child comes to respect and honor the authority of one parent while disregarding the authority of the other. This may be because the alienating parent knows how to play the role of the all-knowing and all-powerful authority better than the targeted parent. Think of how Nora described her husband as having "explained his many rules to me with complete certainty." He didn't doubt the rightness of his opinions, and neither did she or the children.

The sixth and final weapon of influence is the appearance of scarcity. In marketing, this typically involves signaling that there is a limited amount of a product available or that a particular deal is available only on a time-limited basis. With respect to alienation, it refers to the potential for the alienating parent him-/herself to become scarce (i.e., withdrawing their love), creating a heightened demand for their affection. When an object is perceived as scarce or having the potential to be taken away, it becomes more desirable and attractive. Aversion to loss is a powerful mental habit that can be triggered by framing situations in terms of loss, as noted by Lehrer.[15] The alienating parent can activate this trigger simply by becoming aloof or indicating disapproval or disappointment in the child. The fear of loss increases the child's desire for that parent. This can explain what has often been a baffling aspect of alienation, which is that alienated children are eager to please a parent who has rejected them or been uninvolved in raising them. As Nora explains, "It is beyond astounding to me that their father, who never taught them to swim or to ride a bike, never went with them to Boy Scouts, hadn't participated in their lives, has brainwashed them against me." Likewise, Sonya's father abandoned her for an entire year but, shortly after his return, was able to turn her against her mother within a few short hours. The earlier rejection laid the groundwork for the alienation via the principle of scarcity.

Another way that alienating parents were probably able to create the feeling of scarcity is by having a history of cutting off other members of their family when that person displeased them. As noted throughout the stories in this book, the alienating parents had experience ending relationships. The children were therefore aware, on some level, that, should they displease that parent, they, too, could be easily discarded and coldly cast out.

Through these six weapons of influence alienating parents sell their alienation message to their children, creating psychological cohesion with them and disaffection with the targeted parent.

They sell the message the same way that advertisers sell their products to an unsuspecting public. Consumers are generally unaware of the subtle forces at play to create in them a desire for a product they don't want, don't need, and might not be able to afford. The triggers have been pulled and the automatic purchase behavior is activated. The message is bought. The alienation is set into motion.

Because the alienating parents were such effective salesman and were so compelling in their use of the above-described persuasion tactics, it is likely that the legal and mental health professionals who came into contact with them also found them likable and believable. This may explain in part why the alienating parents so often seemed to prevail in court. Few targeted parents reported being understood or supported by the array of mental health and legal professionals that came into contact with their family. Instead, they received quite the opposite. According to one mother, "What I could never get from counselors, legal guardians, or judges was protection from the interference." The alienating parents had successfully sold their message to these professionals as well as the children.

THE LEGAL AND MENTAL HEALTH SYSTEMS: AIDING AND ABETTING THE ALIENATOR

As noted, even an effective salesman with a sticky message needs the proper environment for the message to take off. Most alienating parents required the assistance of legal and mental health professionals for the alienation message to reach its tipping point, and too often they found it. Most of the story submissions mentioned the inability of professionals to prevent the alienation from progressing and the harm from developing following contact with these systems. According to one father, "I haven't seen or heard from my children in eight years, contrary to court orders that, in their best interests, I should care for them part of each week. Over the years I have had five court cases (including an appellate case pro se) across three states, with six attorneys, costing over 60K." At one point, he explains, in response to documented evidence that his ex-wife had filed a false abuse allegation against him, the judge reprimanded her but did not punish or sanction her. "This was hardly the judicial response I had hoped for."

This theme was echoed throughout the stories, affecting both mothers and fathers. Anne noted that her husband was actually rewarded in court with more parenting time despite not having followed the current plan. In one instance, the court-appointed mediator praised George and expressed a wish to have had a father like him. It is no wonder that alienators become so brazen in their disregard for legal agreements and parenting plans. One father reported that he had to go to court repeatedly and "[i]t wasn't until the fifth year that the judge finally saw through Shelly and granted me visitation rights."

It seems clear from the stories that the mental health and legal professionals who served these families were ill prepared to competently and decisively address the problem of parental alienation. This was so for several reasons. First, few attorneys, judges, evaluators, and therapists have received training, especially in differentiating a child who rejects a parent for a good reason (referred to as realistic estrangement) from a child who has been manipulated by one parent to unjustifiably reject the other (referred to as parental alienation or pathological alienation.).

Compounding their lack of training is the presence of a cognitive bias toward believing that most divorces "take two to tango"—that is, both parents are culpable and played a role in the current state of affairs. Clinical reasoning expert Steven Miller describes twelve such cognitive biases and their relevance for parental alienation situations. [16] Moreover, the accusations of the targeted parent that the other parent is turning their child against them can be discounted by the counterbalancing accusations made by the alienating parent. Therapists, evaluators, and judges can throw up their hands and declare, "This is a case of 'he said/she said.' Who can tell what is really going on? It is probably a case of both of them behaving badly." The targeted parent's claims of brainwashing, programming, and parental alienation can sound like psychological mumbo jumbo to those who may prefer a simpler explanation that the rejected parent did something to deserve his/her child's disaffection. This is especially likely if the targeted parent made some mistakes along the way. Even when the mistake is in response to the child's rejection (and hence could not possibly have caused it), it can be pointed to in order to justify judicial inaction.

The judge is likely to be assisted in this resistance to the alienation explanation by the guardian ad litem (GAL) and children's attorney who may be mandated (and inclined anyway) to support the children's claims that they are afraid of or hate the targeted parent. If a custody evaluator is appointed, that person is also likely to conclude that the targeted parent contributed in some way to the problem, due the wildly popular hybrid model in which targeted parents are viewed as "architect[s] of their own rejection," as outlined by sociologist Janet Johnston, a hybrid supporter. [17] The hybrid model is a good example, by the way, of a sticky message that has reached its tipping point in the field of custody evaluations.

With that conclusion, a judge will have no reason to take such bold action as transferring custody or imposing sanctions. A middle-of-the-road response that maintains the status quo (let nature takes it course, let's not rock the boat, the kids will come around when they are ready) is likely to appeal to a judge who is unable or unwilling to parse out the truth or is fearful of backlash from taking decisive steps to intervene.

In some submissions blatant conflicts of interest also appeared to have likely played a role in the exacerbation of the alienation, such as Anna's husband finding a therapist for Sonya who was a friend of a friend (which possibly contributed to her endorsing the father's view that Sonya was a pathological liar), or a targeted parent whose husband's attorney was a campaign contributor to the judge, or a GAL who was the children's former teacher.

As demonstrated throughout the stories, the lack of support and assistance from the legal system compounded the problem, as the alienator was emboldened to ignore court orders while the targeted parent became emotionally and financially drained from the experience. One father sadly recounted, "As the litigation dragged on, a year later, I was not able to emotionally continue the fight."

Thus, the context of the alienation mattered. The professionals who could have properly diagnosed it failed to see it. The attorneys who could have effectively fought it let it languish. The therapists who could have intervened allied themselves with the alienator. The judges who could have imposed orders to rectify the situation took a middle-of-the-road position that in the end allowed the alienation to progress.

IT TAKES A VILLAGE

The community is also a context—a "village," so to speak, that can get pulled into the alienation drama and contribute to it. That is what happened to the targeted parents who wrote their stories for this book. A common experience among targeted parents was being vilified by the other parent, not just to the child and not just to professionals, but also throughout the community. This served multiple purposes, including (perhaps most importantly) shaping and influencing the children via proxy alienators. Joe shared that his ex-wife "approached my closest confidants and told them horrible stories of abuse and mistreatment. The children would spend the next few years hearing about how Daddy beat Mommy and was removed from the house in handcuffs. . . . My name in town would be forever tarnished by Kelly's false accusations." The more people who endorsed the narrative that the alienator was the hero, the child was the victim, and the targeted parent was the villain, the more believable the story would be for the child.

The vilification was also emotionally painful and added to the parent's suffering. As one parent commented, "Another part of the journey for me has been the negative branding I have endured in addition to the grief of losing my children." The vilification compounds the loss for targeted parents by causing them to be cut off from important sources of social and emotional support, denied compassion and understanding, and made to feel as if they don't belong. They were treated as outcasts in the social context in which their children lived.

Joe's experience highlights yet another aspect of this problem. He wrote that "I tried to stay up-to-date with the kid's grades and activities, but when I attended school conferences the expression of pure hatred crossed the faces of the teachers as they looked at me." The vilification and stigmatization that occurred in the community made it difficult for the targeted parents to maintain involvement in their children's lives, which was likely to inadvertently reinforce the negative message that they really didn't love and care about their children.

CHAMPION OF THE ALIENATOR/REPLACEMENT OF THE TARGETED PARENT

In the alienation drama, some people play the very important role of supporting the alienating parent and his or her version of the family drama. These are most typically the parents of the alienating parent and the new spouses/paramours of that parent. These individuals have easy and ongoing access to the children and, for a variety of reasons, they are willing and eager to help sell and support the alienation message.

In several stories the alienator moved a replacement parent into the home very shortly (months, if not weeks) following the end of the marriage. Joe explained, "A few weeks after I was removed from my house, I had heard from a neighbor that Kelly moved a new man into our home." Another man reported, "Just a few weeks after the divorce papers were signed, my ex announced that she was getting remarried. . . . Immediately following the wedding the kids were told to call Dave 'Daddy Dave.'"

One mother wrote that her husband's new wife reassured her daughter that once she turned eighteen "you'll never have to see your mom again. It will be just you and me." The woman continues, "To outsiders this appeared to already be the case, as my daughter's Facebook page omitted any mention or photograph of me but contained over five hundred photographs of her and her stepmother, oftentimes in tightly clutching hugs." Another mother explained that her ex-husband met a woman and after three months became engaged to her and moved into her home with his sons. And Anna tells how her five-year-old daughter Sonya was put under pressure to call her new stepmother "Mom."

These replacement parents are only too willing to engage in indoctrination tactics for their own reasons, such as pleasing their new mate and/or experiencing the gratification of being chosen and adored by the children. In reinforcing the alienation message, they are doubling the pressure on the children and adding to the appearance of the rightness of that parent's position.

The parents of the alienators also played a significant role in the alienation drama by footing the bill for legal expenses, providing a chorus of
support for the alienator's message, and providing emotional and material
support for the alienating parent. One woman wrote about how her son was
controlled and co-opted by his grandfather, a wealthy and powerful man who
could provide the kind of tennis lessons that the son desired: "Hunter's
grandfather was well-off and told him that if he stayed with me it would
destroy his tennis career [the child was ten at the time] because I didn't have
enough money to finance it. On the weekends he was with me, he began
waking up early saying that he had to go practice and that Grand-Dad was
coming to get him. His grandfather began occupying most of his time when
he was supposed to be with me." These "champions" were part of the web of
influence in which the child was caught.

Another member of the chorus of alienation can often be found in the
oldest child, the one who becomes alienated first. In some families, these
children functioned as surrogate alienators, ensuring that the younger and
less alienated children did not soften toward the targeted parents. Knowing
that the surrogate would report back to the alienating parent was in many
instances enough to ensure their compliance with the "program." One mother
wrote, "Since my oldest wouldn't see me, she became part of the alienation
team."

SANDWICHED IN THE LOSS

While the family of the alienator echoed the message and benefited from
extra time with the children, the family members of the targeted parents
suffered. Most of the targeted parents wrote about the pain of losing their
child being that much greater when reflected in the eyes of their own parents.
Formerly beloved grandparents, aunts and uncles, and cousins were shunned,
disregarded, and denigrated. As one man shared, "My entire family has had
limited to no access to my two sons. My sisters and brother, who had been
very close to the boys, were denied any contact. Their calls were ignored, as
were mine. They were turned away at the house, and they were ignored at
social events. They had loved and cherished the boys, and they were totally
cut off. We [had] not only spent holidays and family events together, but also
vacationed and spent other time as a family." Another man lamented, "Not
only have I lost my children, but I [also] have to live with knowing and
hearing about how my children have hurt my family. I have to live with their

grief on top of mine. The weight of this collective grief can be overwhelming at times." These targeted parents struggled with the guilt of having inadvertently inflicted terrible pain on their own parents. In some families, the advanced age and or infirmity of a parent heightened the sense of urgency and despair felt as the alienation deepened.

EROSION OF PARENTAL AUTHORITY

The alienating parents seemed to know exactly which buttons to push and which strings to pull in order to bring the children along, inch by inch down the alienation path. Most likely none said to their child, "I know you love your other parent, but I am going to take that love and turn it into hate and fear." They were probably not so obvious as to reveal the end game. What was happening and where it was headed was painfully obvious only to the targeted parent. They felt the slow and steady erosion of their influence on and relationship with their child. They felt their child slipping away. They felt the erosion of their parental authority. As one mother sadly commented, "Discipline became impossible. My oldest daughter, then thirteen, ran away after a discipline event, never to return. She had called me a bitch during the episode, to which her dad responded that 'maybe that was the right thing to do.'"

Nora shared that when her children came back from visitation with their father, "[T]hey would come back to me as different people from when they left. They came back to my house rude and nasty toward me. They demanded that their father come into the house to adjust the thermostat, since he thought I kept the house too warm."

In the end, there was nothing that these targeted parents could do right and no way to enforce discipline or impose any rules or regulations. One child repeatedly ran away to his father, who gladly harbored him. At the time the boy was ten years old. Any time the child didn't like what the targeted parent had to say, he could summon the other parent, who would be only too willing to "rescue" him. In this way the alienating parent reinforced the message that he was the only parent who mattered, the one "true" and only source of authority in the life of the child.

LIVING IN A MATERIAL WORLD

Yet another common element woven throughout the stories was the influence of material enticements. It probably was not the primary reason that a child became alienated, but it definitely helped the alienator's cause that he or she had more assets and was willing (at least for a while) to shower them on the child.

Obviously money mattered in terms of having the higher-priced attorney (or team, as the case may be). Money mattered for Joe, who lived out of a car while his wife routinely increased child support payments: "I was working harder and longer and it was all going to her. I was trapped." But it also mattered in the day-to-day life of the unfolding alienation drama. One woman wrote that after she tore her knee ligament, she couldn't drive her SUV and borrowed an old car from her father. Her son refused to get in the car: "He said I was poor and that he was embarrassed to be seen with me. He wanted to be cool and if his friends saw me in the car he would be ashamed."

Another way that money helped was in allowing the alienating parent to offer desirable alternatives to visitation/parenting with the targeted parent. Joe explained, "As Kelly realized that her efforts were not working as quickly as she had hoped, she stepped it up a notch. She began to make every one of my custodial weekends a celebration at her house so that the kids would be reluctant to leave her to come be with me. . . . It became a ritual each Thursday night to get a call from one of my kids to ask me if they could stay home that weekend so as not to miss out on what their mother had planned." In this way, the material comforts and benefits of siding with the alienator become part of the context within which the sticky alienation message could take hold in the child.

CONCLUSION

Alienation requires a sticky message (that the targeted parent is unsafe, unloving, and unavailable) that is sold to the children through the effective use of persuasion strategies by the salesman alienating parent and supported through a community context in which the targeted parent has been vilified. When all of these elements are in place, the relationship between the child and the targeted parent is slowly eroded while the child's loyalty and cohesion to the alienating parent is solidified. This is a train wreck waiting to happen. The question taken up in the next chapter is what happens after the train wreck. Can these parents and children find their way back to each other? Can the damage be undone?

Part III

A Targeted Victory

Chapter Six

Coming Home

DAN'S STORY

When my son announced he never wanted to see me again, I felt like something huge and hard was lodged in the center of my chest, but I cannot say that I was surprised. For years I had been witnessing my ex-wife's mission of destroying my relationship with my son Sam and daughter Mindy. I had never heard of Parental Alienation Syndrome (PAS) but knew that whatever was happening in my life was not normal. I spent hours online researching hostile parents, child brainwashing, and manipulation, and began to see articles written on PAS. It had a name! Others were experiencing exactly what I was. I quickly filled my online cart with every book I could on the subject and made an appointment with a psychologist who specialized in PAS.

The psychologist's analysis was a grim one. He agreed that what I described sounded like PAS and warned me to look for continued conflict with their mother, whom he referred to as the alienating parent. He explained that my relationship with the kids was in jeopardy and said my kids would someday be the bearers of deep emotional scars from Parental Alienation Syndrome. I left his office armed with a lot of good information but no clear idea about how I could use it to prevent what was happening. Over the next year I experienced the alienation unfold. It was like a boulder rolling downhill and I had no way of stopping it.

What put that boulder in motion happened a few years prior when my ex-wife had me removed from the home on a false restraining order. Because Tammy had painted a picture of such a horribly abusive and unsafe environment to the authorities, her son from a previous marriage was removed from the house and sent to live with his father. I was thrilled for their justice and hopeful that at least that father and son union would be given a chance.

I helped raise my stepson, Joey, for ten years, and I missed him and worried about his transition. I knew it was time I made amends with his father, the man whom I had treated so poorly over the years. Making the phone call to Chuck and Joey's house was difficult but resulted in my being able to straighten out years of misinformation. We shared stories about the most mundane things and the horrible stories of alleged abuse put on us by the woman we both married. We said our apologies, and at least there was one area of my life I could be at peace with.

The first few weeks my son refused to see me were agonizing for his younger sister and me. Daddy's little girl continued to visit on her own, but she missed her brother terribly and couldn't understand his resistance. She was younger and more innocent and the alienation hadn't gotten to her yet, but I was always waiting for that other shoe to drop. I sensed our time together would be limited.

Over the following months, Sam missed our family vacation, Father's Day, and my birthday. I never went a day without trying to reach him by phone or text message. Most of my attempts were ignored. When I did receive a response, it was usually something along the lines of "I hate you, leave me alone." How does a child have such animosity toward a once-loved parent? What was most troubling was that when asked, he couldn't even tell me why he despised me.

At that time Tammy and I were dealing with a mediator at the court. This case ultimately became too intense for a mediator and we were put in front of a judge to try to rectify the situation. Tammy explained that Sam just didn't want to see me and she couldn't make him. She acknowledged the importance of a father-son relationship and swore she wanted us to have one, but said her hands were tied. The judge ordered us to see a family therapist to repair Sam's and my problems.

At our first appointment with Fred, the psychologist, Tammy showered this new therapist with compliments. She told him he came highly recommended by her friends and she knew he would do wonders for us. For an hour the words were tumbling out of her mouth, all of which were lies. She painted a picture in which everything she did was fantastic and all that was bad in her life was someone else's fault. I got the sense that she was on a mission to win Fred over so his testimony could be used against me in court and that she really did not care about repairing my relationship with my son. Upon leaving our session we agreed on a time to meet the following week; this time Sam would be involved. I was so thrilled about seeing my son again, I didn't care about the venue it would take place.

The next week I arrived at the psychologist's appointment a few minutes early, walked up to the second floor, and had a seat in the waiting room. A large widow overlooked the parking lot, so I positioned myself in front of it, eagerly awaiting my son's arrival. It had been months since I had seen or spoken with him. My ex-wife pulled up and stepped out of the car; then the passenger door opened and her boyfriend, Peter, climbed out. Sam was not in sight. Apparently Sam didn't want to see me and they didn't feel it was right to make the boy do something he didn't want to.

The sessions went on this way for ten months and numerous letters were written to the court by the therapist. Over time, as Fred witnessed more of Tammy's actions, the letters began to sway in my favor. She was a master manipulator, but I was patient. I believed that if she were given enough rope, she would eventually hang herself.

In time she quit the court-ordered therapy altogether, saying it was too stressful for her and not helping the situation. Tammy told Fred that she was in fear of being in the same room with me. Fred saw directly through that accusation and added it in his next report to the court.

In a year's time she was unable to get my son to one session with me. Fred did, however, see the kids without me, on her time. He wrote that my son had no genuine fear of me and could see no reason for such behavior by him. With complete certainty, he also stated that in his thirty years of practice he had seen many cases that looked like Parental Alienation Syndrome but had never seen one that was so clearly it. And also with complete certainty, I knew it was time to go back to court to fight for a change in custody.

Getting a date for such a hearing took long months. It is said that time is an alienator's best friend and I feared that was true. My son was gone out of my life and I felt my daughter, Mindy, following in his tracks. I had to be polite and precise in everything I did. I walked on eggshells, as I feared that even normal parental discipline could be misunderstood by my ex-wife or serve as ammunition for her to accuse me of abuse. I had lost my parental authority. I was so fearful of losing my daughter that I gave in to all of Mindy's requests. I worried about what this would do to my daughter in the long run, but I was desperate not to lose her. Tammy continued to woo

Mindy with bribes and rewards, and again I was helpless to stop her from keeping my child from me.

Tammy knew court was coming up and something drastic had to happen in her favor. On a Friday night I went to pick up our daughter for her weekend visit. Our meeting location was at the police station to assure that there would be no incidents. While I waited in my car for Mindy to make the switch of vehicles, I became nauseous when I noticed that she wasn't getting out of her mom's car. When she finally emerged, I got out and said, "Come on honey, let's go." That's when she informed me that she was not coming with me and never wanted to see me again. It was my son's situation all over again!

Frantic at the thought of losing another child to PAS, I reached for her, and her mother hollered for Mindy to run to the police station, as if she were in danger. A literal tug of war over Mindy erupted between Tammy and me, and Mindy was caught in the middle. Mindy stumbled and scratched her knee on the ground, and Tammy dramatically announced that I was abusing our daughter. I calmly let go and walked into the police station, knowing they would follow me. I had been around this woman long enough to know that if I looked at her cross-eyed, she would try to press charges against me.

While in the foyer of the state trooper barracks, Tammy accused me of threatening her right there in front of the officer's desk. This was her chance and she was trying to bury me. The officers placed us in separate rooms, me in one and my daughter and her mother in another. It sickened me to think of what must have been going through Mindy's young mind. We were all questioned for an hour and asked to write our statements.

Tammy demanded a restraining order and thankfully was denied one because her story didn't make sense. Panicked that her plan hadn't worked, Tammy concocted another tale. In this story I had picked Mindy up and dropped her to the ground out of anger and Mindy hit her head and needed to go to the hospital immediately! The officer pointed out that a head injury was not mentioned in her original statement and when a bandage was offered to Mindy for the small scrape on her knee, Mindy refused it, saying she was "fine." Tammy insisted that she wanted to take her to the hospital and now, by ambulance.

The police refused to provide an ambulance but said that since it was my custodial time I could take my daughter to the hospital to resolve the matter. I scooped up my daughter and she willingly hopped in the car with me to go to the emergency room. At the ER I was greeted by a nice doctor who gave

Mindy a clean bill of health. We also spoke with a woman from social services. She was investigating an anonymous call about a little girl being abused at the police station during a custodial pickup. Tammy had just enough time during the car ride to the hospital to make that call. After a long discussion with the officers on duty that evening, social services decided it was a nonincident and allowed me to leave the hospital with my daughter around midnight. We slept in the next morning and I took her out for pancakes.

Remarkably, Mindy's spirits were fine the next day. She was happily playing at a friend's house when I got the first phone call from my son in over fourteen months. Sam phoned me to say that I was dead to him and how dare I beat his sister the way that I had the night before at the police station. He announced that his mom's boyfriend, Peter, was now his father and not me. For days afterward I received harassing text messages from both Tammy and Peter saying I was going to lose custody of the children and Peter was going to adopt them. Like most things they suggested, this made no sense, but it was the new angle they were trying.

Mindy and I had a vacation planned together and I realized while traveling that her mother had loaded a tracking device onto our daughter's iPod. When we switched the towns we were visiting, Tammy accused me of kidnapping our daughter. That was the second time I got a phone call from Sam. He was demanding that I return his sister immediately!

Our day in court finally came. I hadn't slept in days. I was on the stand for hours, as was our therapist Fred and Tammy's first husband. The evidence against her was mounting and the only defense she had was that the psychologist was biased. My lawyer reminded Tammy that the psychologist was of her choosing and she had been quite pleased with him in the beginning. She tried to play the abuse card, but that was dismissed for lack of evidence.

My lawyer and I tried our hardest to not have the kids testify that day, but we lost that request. There was my son on the stand. I was seeing him for the first time in eighteen months and he was dressed up waiting to testify against me. When Sam and Mindy left the judge's chambers, Sam was in hysterics. I knew how I felt, how hard this day was. I couldn't even imagine how difficult it must be for him, and I wondered how Tammy could put our child through this. Tammy ran to his aid and shot her head back at me sternly and asked, "Are you happy now?!"

No decision was made that day and we were scheduled to resume a few weeks later. The wait was agonizing. Our new court date was the week before Christmas and I feared what the holidays would be like that year for all of us. I dressed that morning in my red holiday tie and headed off to the courthouse. I asked my lawyer if he had any vibe as to how this was going to go, and he admitted he had no idea. He told me it was a tricky case and that most men don't get their kids. And to make matters worse for me, I lived in another state. My lawyer explained it was rare for a judge to move children to another state.

Standing in front of the judge, my knees nearly collapsed beneath me when he awarded primary custody to me. He proceeded to scold Tammy for her role in separating a father and his son. His words, though wonderful, were wasted on us both. I couldn't comprehend what had just happened and began to sob while Tammy ran out of the courtroom dry heaving. The judge continued with his speech.

I brought my children home on December 26. They had a week to get accustomed to their new living arrangements before school resumed after the holiday break. They never set foot back in their old school again. They didn't have the opportunity to say good-bye to friends or clean out their lockers. They were plucked out of their old lives and inserted into this new one.

They came to my car at the final drop-off with two bags each. A small plastic shopping bag with some cloths and a large duffle bag filled with framed pictures of their mother and her boyfriend. They came with no winter jackets, but enough photos to wallpaper a room. I had no doubt that the judge had made the right decision for this family.

I've had Sam and Mindy living with me for a year and a half now. It hasn't been easy, but we're making it work. I am a single father of two teenage kids. I'm packing lunches, doing homework, and taking my daughter dress shopping. By all accounts my kids are happy and adjusting remarkably well. I don't take a single moment for granted. One day Sam and I were in the kitchen peeling potatoes together and I had to excuse myself. Having him with me, doing an ordinary task, brought me to tears.

I tell them I love them every night before bed and they never say it back to me. Although that cuts deep within me, I take comfort in the fact that my fifteen-year-old son still calls me Daddy and wakes me up when he has a nightmare. I know my kids love me.

As for their mother, she has not learned a single thing by having all three of her children taken from her. Anonymous calls about me are still being reported to youth and family services. None have ever been found to be true. Tammy and her boyfriend reported our family psychologist to the state for malpractice. An online petition was created to "Bring home Sam and Mindy." Close to two hundred people from around the country signed this plea to have the kids removed from their "highly abusive" father. I have never met any of these people, and yet they all supposedly know me.

The nonsensical chatter can swarm around me and I no longer care. I'm too busy being "Daddy" to my kids.

GAIL'S STORY

The loss of my daughter cast a shadow over my life. It dulled the taste of the most delicious food. It made even the most beautiful artwork or sunset less vibrant and compelling. I had no interest in socializing, as every conversation reminded me of the hole in my life and in my heart. Some days I felt like a zombie, the walking dead, moving through my life but apart from my life, less engaged and involved because of the never-ending sense of loss. The dull ache was with me every moment, like the beating of my heart.

If I wasn't at work, I spent nearly every waking minute thinking about how to rescue my daughter. My husband and I spoke to several attorneys, all of whom strongly discouraged us from seeking legal remedy given how old my daughter was (seventeen at the time) and the fact that she had "voluntarily" moved in with her father. We spoke to experts in cults and considered kidnapping her and deprogramming her. We looked into every program and option that we knew of and couldn't find one that we thought stood a chance of working with her.

We believed with all of our hearts that our best chance of getting her back was to wait for her father to suffocate and stifle her so intensely that she would rebel out of her need to exercise her autonomy. We knew that Lila was a very strong-willed person despite her subservience to her father. We believed that with me out of the picture and her father, Jerry, currently unmarried, the only person he would have available for him to control and manipulate would be Lila. We bet that she had too strong a desire to be her own person to stand for that too long.

While waiting for Lila to have her fill of her father, we did everything we could to let her know that we loved and missed her and would accept her back anytime, anywhere, with no questions asked. One of my most consistent anti-alienation strategies was to call my daughter every single day at 4:15 in the afternoon. I was walking the short distance from my office to the subway. I believed that this time was the window between her coming home from school and her father coming home from work. I knew that he had convinced her to forgo nearly all of her extracurricular activities, so she would most likely be available. Every single day, no matter how painful it was, no matter how sad I felt, no matter how devastating it was to hear her voice message, I called her. Nearly always the machine clicked on. Just hearing her voice on the message was a knife in my heart, I missed her so much. Hiding my emotions, I always left a loving message for her with the hopes that hearing my voice would spark a memory in her to connect her with our love for each other. I used those messages to let her know about upcoming family events so that she could be included should she want to (almost never) and to let her know that I wanted to see her. I was usually done with the message by the time I arrived at the subway station.

About once every six to eight weeks, she answered the phone. During those times I stayed on the call as long as she was willing, sometimes walking thirty blocks or more. When she answered, shocked as I was, I tried to keep my tone calm. We chatted about what was going on with her in school or in her social life or about movies and current events. She never allowed me to pin her down for an actual visit, she never explained why she had moved out or cut me off, she never even really acknowledged that we had virtually no relationship. I usually didn't press her to explain herself because I understood that she probably didn't know why she was doing what she was doing and that to make her come up with a reason would only hurt and anger her. To say that I walked on tiptoes during those rare calls is an understatement. I was so careful not to say anything to upset her. At the same time, I was walking on a cloud as I had the rare and delightful experience of connecting with my lost child. For a few moments I felt like a mother again.

I also showed up at her various places of employment to see if I could give her a quick hug and chat. She was periodically receptive to me, but never agreed to make a plan to spend time with me or talk to me about what was going on. Sometimes when I visited, she was brusque and showed no emotion toward me. Those were very hard moments indeed.

I reached out to the parents of her friends and acquaintances (some of whom were my friends and some of whom were not). None offered to speak to Lila on my behalf, feeling it wasn't their place or that they, too, would be shunned by her if they shared their true feelings about her treatment of me.

Another approach was to speak with the guidance counselor of her school begging him to offer her counseling and to encourage her to let me back into her life. I wrote lengthy explanations for what was going on in our family, sharing my concern for Lila. I have no idea if the guidance counselor read what I wrote, but shortly afterward Jerry convinced Lila that her counselor was not doing a good job and she switched to a new one. The new one happened to be someone a friend of mine knew and I asked that friend to write a letter to the new counselor on my behalf, but she never did.

My husband and I wracked our brains day and night to find ways to reach out to Lila, to spark in her a desire and recognition of her need for her mother. No idea was too far-fetched for us to consider, but we had to have some confidence that it would make things better, not worse.

It was during this time that I sought out counseling with an expert in cults. I tried to learn as much as I could about the experience Lila was going through from her perspective and to understand how and why people leave cults. My husband and I immersed ourselves in learning as much as we could about this experience in order to maximize our chances of having Lila return to us.

Lila began her first semester of college in the fall of 2006, about one hour away from my home. I immediately began sending her care packages filled with gift cards, magazines, and small items that I knew she liked. My goal was to show her that I remembered her tastes and interests and to forge some kind of connection with her. Soon after, she called me one day and asked me to come visit. It was all I could do to not speed all the way there, so eager was I to see my child. I have a picture from that day on my refrigerator of the two of us hugging. I don't know who was holding on more strongly, her or me.

Lila arranged for an all-day road trip with two friends, so there was no chance to discuss anything too personal. Part of me was screaming inside, "Does this mean you are going to be back in my life????? Is it over??" but I tried to keep my cool and stay in the moment, enjoying the longest time together we had had together in over two years. When we finally said good-bye at the end of the day, I was fairly certain that she would not disappear again.

I was right.

We spoke all of the time that first year she was in college. Usually she would be the one to call me and invite me down for a visit. No matter what I was doing, I would jump in the car and be there within the hour. That year I lived in fear of speeding tickets! Too soon came the end of her first year in school. I was worried about whether she would return to her father's for the summer and I wouldn't see her, but I was afraid of bringing up the subject with her, as our mode of operating had been to not make manifest the obvious fact that she had disappeared for over two years. Shortly before the end of the semester she asked me to come help her clean out her room and pack up for the summer.

I remarked to my husband that she probably knew that she wouldn't see me again until the fall and therefore wanted a long visit to say good-bye. I was grateful to have this last visit with her and we spent the day organizing her belongings and packing her car to take all of her stuff back to her father's. We hugged and kissed good-bye, and I reminded her that she could call me any time and that I wanted nothing more than to continue to see her and have her be a part of my life. I told her she was wanted at home and we would always have a place for her.

Over the next few weeks she did keep in touch with me. She drove the hour from her father's house to mine to hang out with me (unbeknownst to him). She started to share with me that things were not going so well with her father. Inside I was jumping for joy, but outside I was calmly expressing my motherly concern. I tried to contain my hope and excitement that perhaps the thing I had dreamed of for so long was finally coming to pass.

A few times when she was with me, he would call or text her demanding that she return immediately, and I could sense her fear and nervousness when she responded to him. As always, I reassured her that she didn't have to go back to him. I ventured to say a few times that he was an angry person who wanted to control her and she didn't have to stand for it anymore. I sensed a receptivity in her to my feedback and increased the frequency and honesty of my observations and concerns.

One day she called and I felt that there was an opening within her to my understanding of what had happened between us. As we talked, I shared with her my perception of what she had given up to please her father (basically everything that was important to her) and the price she had paid to keep him in her life. I let her know that I believed in no uncertain terms that he did not want what was best for her and that he was not capable of sharing her with me. What kind of father demands that his child cut off her mother, I asked her? Is that love? I held nothing back as she listened to the torrent of words and feelings pour out of me.

A neighbor had been sitting by while this was going on, and when the conversation was over I turned to her and apologized for exposing her to this intense emotional outburst, but I explained that I basically had been waiting for a decade to be this honest with my daughter about what her father had done to her. Later that day Lila came to visit and we hugged closely. I felt her heart opening to me. She noticeably jumped when her cell phone indicated a text message from her father: "You have 45 minutes."

She told me that he was quite angry and dissatisfied with her because she hadn't sold her horse at what she knew to be an inflated price. He also knew that she had been spending time with me. She turned to me, confused and scared, and I told her that she didn't have to go back. "You can do this," I told her. "You don't need to let him hurt you anymore." She also called a therapist whom she had seen a few times with her father (this person had been her father's individual therapist first and later began to see them jointly). The therapist told Lila, "You know how angry your father gets. You really should get back to him quickly." When I heard this, I was furious and explained to my daughter that this woman did not have *her* best interests at heart. She was functioning as a protector of her father.

Lila did not go back that day.

A few hours later the phone rang and I was informed by the policeman on the other end of the line that Lila's father had asked that she be arrested for grand theft auto because she refused to return the car she was driving—a car that he had bought as a gift for her. I calmly explained to the officer that no one had requested that she return the vehicle, but my daughter would gladly do so the following day. There had been no need for a call to the police except as a way to terrorize and punish Lila.

She brought some friends with her the next day (as arranged with the police) to return the car and pick up her belongings. When she arrived, her father was nowhere in sight and all of her possessions had been locked in a storage shed on his property. Eventually she hired an attorney to retrieve her belongings. A few weeks later, she found out through an acquaintance that her father had arranged to have her horse put down—without even letting her say good-bye (and for questionable reasons).

More than I could ever say to Lila, her father's actions (trying to have her arrested, locking up her possessions, putting her horse down) revealed to her the true nature of her father. He showed himself as the vindictive, mean-spirited person he was, and from that day forward she has had no contact with him. Although saddened by what her father put her through, I am thankful each day that I got my daughter back. No child should have to learn the lessons that my daughter learned—that the person she trusted exploited that trust, and that his desire to hurt and control me was more important to him than her need to love and be loved by both of her parents.

SETH'S STORY

Who would have thought when I got married to Shari that I would get divorced, and if I got divorced, that Shari would brainwash our daughters—Ava and Jackie—against me? Who knew what alienation was; who would have thought that Shari would use our children as pawns for her own purposes against me? All I know is, the worst nightmare happened to me when my ex-wife wanted to get back at me for getting involved with another woman.

As I wrestled with staying or leaving the marriage, I learned that Shari shared with my mother that she was going to take me to the cleaners and ruin my life. I learned that ruining my life meant turning Ava and Jackie against me and creating one of the most draining financial and mental experiences I had to face in my life.

In a period of two months, I went from being an active and loved father to being accused of physically and emotionally abusing my daughters. My girls called me a loser, stopped talking/e-mailing with me, did not want to see me, and, sadly enough, even stopped interacting with my mother. I agreed to not protest Shari's moving back to the town she grew up in a state away because she said that she and the girls would be happier there. It was close enough that I could continue my parenting and I hoped that agreeing to the plan would improve my standing with Ava and Jackie. I now see the move as part of Shari's plan to completely cut them off from me.

When this all started, I was in shock, could not sleep well, and became depressed. I missed my daughters and being an involved parent to them. What helped me is that I am a very persistent person with a lot of fight in me. I finally focused on what I needed to do in order to turn this situation around. I started to read books on alienation and reached out to professionals in the field.

One of the first books I read was Alec Baldwin's *A Promise to Ourselves* (2009). I remember Alec talking about how, because his daughter did not want to see or speak to him, he felt like she was dead, even though she was alive. That was how I was starting to feel and I vowed to myself that I was going to do everything possible not to let that become my reality, to not let my loving relationship with my daughters fade into oblivion.

I also read Baker's *Adult Children of Parental Alienation Syndrome: Breaking the Ties that Bind*. The most important message in that book for me was that the adults who had been alienated as children felt that their targeted parent could have fought harder for them. That stayed with me during my terrible ordeal and remains my mantra to this day. I believe that alienated children are saying to their parent, "Look, I was messed up. I was taught to hate you. It was not my fault. Why didn't you stick it out, why did you leave me?" I learned that when a parent gives in to the alienation—either because they lose the will to keep fighting or because they think it is the right thing to do—it will feel like abandonment by the child, especially because the alienating parent is trying to convince the child that the other parent doesn't love or want them. So I felt that if I gave in to my children, they would have a reason to believe that I gave up on them.

I was fortunate to have an excellent attorney who knew how to frame what was happening so that judge would be convinced there was a serious problem in my family. Without that, I think my case would have been doomed to being a spiral of wasted money, time, and energy, and a bad conclusion.

I was also very fortunate to have in my local area (ironically, the area that my ex-wife insisted on moving to) nationally recognized experts in identifying and treating parental alienation. Too often therapists claim to know how to treat parental alienation, but in reality do not. The first therapist I met did not get it, but thankfully I found one who did. Without a court-appointed therapist who really knew what they were doing, I would have been sunk. The therapist appointed to my case was able to observe the alienation tactics by my ex and submit reports to the judge. My ex was fined, found in contempt, almost put in jail, and lost custody twice. Both times my girls behaved as if they were miserable with me, but I was assured by the therapist that the time we spent together would be helpful in the long run.

It was very painful and challenging to deal with them during this time. My once loving daughters refused to speak to me and acted as if they wanted nothing to do with me. I got a lot of support from the therapists who said to hold on to the belief that my girls were just acting and that deep down they still loved me. If not for that, I would have gone crazy and might have responded to them with anger and blown any chance I had of repairing our relationship. I tried my best to love them and accept them and behave as if nothing was wrong.

My ex's true intentions were revealed when she filed a bogus restraining order against me so she could cut off all contact. I believe that during this time she was working hard to convince Ava and Jackie that I did not love them, want to be with them, or support them. I kept fighting her in court by filing orders to show cause against her for interfering in my relationship with them and not facilitating their relationship with me, as she had agreed to and as the judge expected her to do. When I would become frustrated and despairing, my lawyer would say to me, "Let her hang herself with her actions; the judge sees she is alienating the girls." After a year and half of my having no contact with Ava and Jackie, the judge finally enforced therapy for us with no further delays or interference from Shari.

I remember when the therapist asked Ava, my older daughter, whether she read the e-mails I had continued to send during the period of no contact, even though she never responded to them. Ava admitted that she had been reading them, and the therapist pointed out to me later in private that Ava's response showed that she still loved me and was torn between showing her true feelings for me and showing hatred as she had been taught. That really helped motivate me to keep fighting for my girls. I realized that I needed to free them from the brainwashing—I could not give up.

Near the conclusion of therapy, I started to have weekly dinners with Ava and Jackie, which led to regular visitations after the judge signed off on the therapist's recommendation. I was finally able to have regular contact with my girls! I have been told by the professionals that regular contact helps the alienated child slowly break free from the brainwashing. Without regular contact, I do not think I would have made positive progress with my daughters.

Once regular visits began, I decided to move to the same town as Shari and the girls to show my daughters that I loved them, and to make visits easier. I also wanted to demonstrate that I would never abandon them and that I would do whatever it took to have them in my life. At the time, I wondered whether this was the right move. I was worried about how Shari and her parents would react, and whether that would influence the feelings of my girls toward me.

I think my ex resented my moving to her hometown and probably felt that I was invading her space. I think Ava and Jackie followed their mother's lead and acted as if they were not happy with my move. And yet one of the happiest moments I had was when my girls slept over for the time in my new apartment, and then Ava asked me to pick up her friends and her from a party and drive them home. I actually teared up in the car being with all of them and actually getting to know her friends. I felt like a real father again, doing carpools and sharing a moment/memory with one of my daughters and her friends.

Moments like these, and the belief that Ava and Jackie needed me even if they couldn't show it, kept me going and helped me stay strong. And I needed mental toughness, because there were many negative moments yet to come.

Both Ava and Jackie were led to believe that the judge, the therapists, and anyone else who took my side were paid off by me. When I won custody for the second time because Shari was once again in violation of a court order, Ava went to the courthouse to file a restraining order against me (something she had seen her mother do earlier). I remember going to Shari's house to get the girls and the police showing up to tell me that I could not see them due to the restraining order. I asked the police officer to have Ava come talk to me. I wanted to ask her why she was doing this. She finally came out and said, "I will want nothing to do with you when I am eighteen [which was a year and half away]." I was flabbergasted that she continued to feel that way, since by then she had been staying with me every other weekend and we had been sharing some positive moments together.

Besides filing the restraining order, my daughter also filed criminal charges against me, saying that I had violated the restraining order. I had to endure a day and a half of being in jail until I was arraigned. I could not believe Ava had me put in jail. How sick is that? What helped me get through this challenge was reminding myself that she did not mean it, and that I needed to keep fighting for her or I would lose her forever.

When the presiding judge heard what my daughter had done, she ordered both girls into foster care. Things became very chaotic suddenly, as we had judges from two states involved, as well as foster care agencies from both states. Shari and her parents were blaming me and telling my girls that I wanted to put them into foster care and ruin their lives. I had my doubts as to what the right move was, although therapists and friends told me to let them to go to foster care so they finally could learn that they could not control the situation. I was torn. I could either sit back and let the process happen or do something to stop it, because while the majority of people were saying to let them go into foster care, I believed that this was too high a price for them to pay. I had visions of them languishing in foster care with no love, their lives ruined. And the person they would blame for all of this would be me. I feared that I would lose them forever.

With this in mind, I felt that I had to stop the battle. I decided after all the time, fight, money, and love I had for my girls, I could not let them go into foster care. I pleaded with Shari to promise to help me improve my relationship with Ava and Jackie. I begged her to free them mentally so that they could enjoy a relationship with me. I told her that it was not fair to them to go into foster care. Shari agreed. She said that she would help. I didn't know whether I should believe her, but I was desperate to prevent Ava and Jackie from going into foster care. I hoped that Shari would keep her word.

I let the presiding judge know that a new visitation schedule had been worked out between Shari and me, and that, therefore, there was no need for the girls to be placed in foster care. Of course, I had no way of knowing whether my ex would be true to her word and follow the new agreement. I had to take that chance because I felt even though my girls might still act like they hated me, that was still better than their going into foster care and blaming me for the rest of their lives.

It has been four months since this incident, and during the summer, Ava had a weekly dinner with me. (Jackie was in camp.) Ava actually shares what is going on in her life. I speak to her daily and we converse about her day and life events. No more yes/no answers. I asked her, when Jackie comes home from camp, does she think both of them can sleep over at my apartment every other week? She told me, "Let us think about it." But the most impressive response I have received from Ava, who just a few months ago wanted nothing to do with me when she was eighteen, was "I cannot mentally get you out of my head," and she has agreed to let me take her to visit a college she is seriously considering. I will be involved in her college admission process, something I would have never thought was possible just a little while ago. I feel like a parent again even though I was robbed of years of true, loving fatherhood.

I realize my relationship with Ava and Jackie is still, and will probably always be, a work in process due to the mental and emotional damage they have suffered, but I need to remind myself to be persistent, realize it is not their fault, and remember that the most important thing is not to give up.

CLAUDIA'S STORY

During the disintegration of our twenty-year marriage, my former spouse promised to take our two children away from me and find a "surrogate mother" for them. He ultimately divorced me and followed through with these threats.

After nine years of complete alienation, I was contacted by my twenty-four-year-old daughter, Jocelyn. She was angry and blaming me for her present dilemma: she had been accepted into a competitive six-year doctor of pharmacy degree program and didn't know how she was going to pay for it. Jocelyn said that she really wished that I had not "stolen" her college fund (an alienation lie told to her by her father). She was also buried in credit card debt and did not know how to dig herself out. The pharmacy program required full-time attendance and substantial out-of-pocket tuition charges not covered by student loans. Jocelyn explained that the most that she could manage as a full-time student was a part-time job. At that rate, it would be impossible for her to keep up with the credit card payments. She planned to use personal loans to cover the out-of-pocket portion of the tuition.

Jocelyn's credit card troubles did not come as a surprise to me. As a matter of fact, the handwriting was on the wall years earlier. Part of her father's alienation strategy was to "buy" our children away from me. My protests fell on deaf ears as he gave them credit cards in their early teens—without any instruction in financial responsibility. They were lead to believe that money grows on trees, and that Daddy was a big, happy money tree, while Mommy was nothing but a "killjoy" for believing that their father was setting them up to become financially irresponsible adults. He was also setting them up for him to be able to financially manipulate them by threatening to cut off these funds if they did not follow his alienation program. So, I wondered, where was her father now that she had these inevitable financial woes?

My daughter made it clear on the phone that day that she was not willing to discuss him with me or to ask him for help.

Part of me felt overjoyed. It was a dream come true to hear from Jocelyn after all those years of no response to my many communications. Maybe she still loved me! Maybe she had missed me! Maybe I hadn't been replaced by a "surrogate mother"! Maybe she needed her real mom!

Another part of me felt suspicious. Is my daughter looking to rekindle our relationship or is she just looking for another money tree? After all, she is not only my child but also her father's child. If she takes after him, she will only desire a relationship with me as long as I am useful to her. The moment that I outlive my usefulness, she will put me out of her life like putting out the trash.

I was confused and conflicted about how to proceed. I knew how I felt about her—I loved her with every fiber of my being. I never stopped loving her, even when she acted unloving toward me, for I always believed that it was truly just that—an act—to please her father. Yet I didn't know how she presently felt about me.

While I wanted to help her because she is, biologically, my daughter, I wasn't sure if it would be wise for me to do so, since she is, relationally, a stranger. When I knew her, she was a child. I didn't know this adult person that she had become. I didn't know if her father was still using her as an instrument to hurt me. I didn't want to get scammed.

On the other hand, I believed that it would have been a grave disservice to Jocelyn to unjustly ascribe her father's negative character traits to her. After all, she is also my child, and I know that I had worked hard to instill my values in her during her twelve years of pre-alienation upbringing. I just couldn't believe that all of the effort that I had put into her moral development could totally have been obliterated by alienation programming. My input must still be there inside of her somewhere, buried, but not eradicated. Perhaps I could help her to excavate and to reconnect with that part of herself. Then, possibly, the good could have a chance, in the end, to win out over the "evil" programming.

I decided to err in Jocelyn's favor, to give her the benefit of the doubt, to help her to seize the opportunity to train for her dream career. Also, selfishly, as a parent, I wanted to be able to rest easy, knowing that my child is equipped to fend for herself after I am gone. So, I asked her if she would like to meet me in a public place to work together to develop a financial plan to pay for her tuition and to pay off her credit cards. I was surprised when she preferred that I come to her apartment.

The thought occurred to me that I might be getting lured into an ambush orchestrated by her father. As a precaution, I notified my family of Jocelyn's address and instructed them to call the police if they did not hear from me right after my meeting with her.

The security system in her building required me to buzz her apartment from the lobby to announce my arrival, and then required her to buzz the lobby back to unlock the security door. Once inside the building, I located her apartment and found her door wide open, with her standing just inside. Though Jocelyn glared at me with cold, angry eyes, I stepped inside, embraced her, and felt a reluctant, chilly hug in return. At least she did not push me away. I perceived that to be a good sign, even though it wasn't the reception that I would have fantasized about during our long separation. Instead, I drew courage from the parental alienation research that I had done in preparation for this very moment. I told myself that my daughter was like a person possessed, and that I was actually looking into the eyes of her resident demon, not the eyes of my child. I told myself that I would need to perform an exorcism, of sorts, to purge her of that demon known as Parental Alienation Syndrome in order to free her to regain control of her own thoughts and emotions. In the meantime, I needed to be careful not to confuse the child with the demon, and to be mindful to react to each of them individually and appropriately.

I knew that I had my work cut out for me. I felt in way over my head. I was petrified of doing or saying the wrong things—things that would solidify the programming instead of weakening it. Yet I was more petrified of doing nothing. To do nothing would be to abandon her, to just hand her over to this demon. I told myself that I am her mother, that it is my job to protect her.

These were the thoughts that were swirling around in my mind during our first meeting. As Jocelyn anxiously moved in wide circles around me that day, as if I were a leper, we began to hammer out a financial plan. We also began to establish the boundaries that each of us required of our newfound relationship.

Jocelyn made it clear that our reconnection must remain a secret from her father, or else he would terminate his relationship with her, and then her brother would follow suit. She further made it clear that questions about her father and her brother (who has been totally alienated from me for thirteen years) were off limits. I understood that the loyalty bind that such questions would create for her was part of her alienation programming, so I diligently respected this boundary.

The payback has been that, over time, she began to spontaneously volunteer limited information about her father and her brother. At those times, I keep in mind that these are just moments when the demon has let its guard down and my child is free to divulge her own true thoughts and feelings. I cherish these windows of opportunity to have "my girl" back, but I accept that they are fleeting—at least for now. Invariably, the demon rears its ugly head again, and my daughter abruptly says, "I don't want to talk about this anymore." So, we immediately change the subject, and we never revisit it unless and until she initiates it again.

I never want to make her regret opening up to me by bringing up a confided subject outside of its moment. I made that mistake once, and her surprised reaction was "I told you that?" It was as if the content of that particular moment was once again locked away in a vault inside of her memory—a vault that is not accessible to her at will, but only when it has been inadvertently left unguarded by the demon.

So I have learned that the progress of renewing our relationship must be gauged by her pace, and not according to my or anyone else's timeline. I am finding that this approach works best for Jocelyn. For me, it is not always an easy task, because I am starved for information about my son. However, I believe that, as her parent, I must put her needs above my own in order to be able to help her—at least for now.

As far as my boundaries are concerned, I made it clear that although I wanted nothing more than to rebuild a relationship with her, I was not willing to simply pick up where we had left off. Specifically, I would no longer be willing to tolerate the abuse that she was programmed to hurl at me in order to please her alienating parent. So, whenever she raised her voice at me or otherwise reflexively exhibited any of the old bad behaviors, I told her that we would have to postpone the rest of the interaction until she was ready to engage with me respectfully.

At those times when I ended phone conversations to assert this boundary, I feared that I might never hear from her again. But within a matter of minutes, she called me back with a reformed attitude. It confirmed for me that she values having a relationship with me enough to take my boundary needs into consideration and to adjust her behavior accordingly. At those times, I perceived that she was accessing the buried respect that she once had for me before she was drafted into her alienating father's campaign of denigration against me—like she was reconnecting with that part of herself that she once had to "amputate" in order to please him. At times like that I feel hopeful—when I see evidence that she is learning to control the demon instead of letting it control her, when I say to myself, "That's my girl."

All in all, it has been a painfully slow process, and it definitely has had its ups and downs. For example, during my daughter's third year of pharmacy school, a "White Coat Ceremony" was held to formally present each student with the "uniform" of his/her future vocation. She never told me about this event, and when I learned about it after the fact (on Facebook!), I asked her if family members had been permitted to attend. She matter-of-factly replied that her father and her brother had been there. Then, on second thought, she asked, "Why? You wouldn't have wanted to come, would you?" When I replied affirmatively, she seemed surprised, even though I am the one help-ing her with her tuition! I think that it was the first time that she questioned her programmed belief that it is only her father's place, and not her mother's place, to be present at such milestones in her life. Nonetheless, I will have to prepare myself for the probability that I will not be invited to attend her graduation in two years.

In the meantime, next year there is another major milestone coming up in her life that will be even more painful for me to be excluded from—her wedding. Apparently, her father left it up to his girlfriend (the designated "surrogate mother") to announce our daughter's engagement in the local newspapers. She entirely omitted me from the announcement and worded it as though she is my daughter's birth mother. Apparently, they plan to keep up this charade at the wedding, and my daughter seems resigned to go along with it. She can't invite me or any of her other maternal relatives, since her father does not know that she has rekindled a relationship with us.

I validated the horrendous no-win position that my daughter is in by telling her that no child should ever be forced to choose between parents. I let her know that as heartbreaking as it will be for me to not attend her wedding, I would rather make those sacrifices than pressure her to stand up to her father at the risk of losing him and her brother. It's bad enough that one of her parents is forcing her to choose; she doesn't need both parents pressuring her. My daughter thanked me for being willing to make that sacrifice in order to spare her. I silently wondered whether I was a hero or an enabler.

To date, my daughter and I have been reunited for four years. We are making slow but steady progress in some areas of our rebuilt relationship, and no apparent progress in other areas. She is not ready to risk being disowned by her father and her brother as a consequence of openly asserting her right to have a relationship with me. They still have a rigid "us or her" mentality. Therefore, I must settle for bits and pieces of my daughter—those parts of her that are not monopolized by them or cut off from herself. In many respects, I must settle for being a closeted, second-class parent. For now, these crumbs of a relationship are a welcome relief from the starvation of having been completely alienated from her for so many years.

Although my daughter gave me an icy reception at our first meeting, her good-bye was noticeably warmer, leading me to believe that the ice had been broken. Therefore, it was quite disheartening when she again greeted me coldly at our next meeting. This pattern of icier hellos than good-byes continued for many visits as she wrestled with the demon. Over time, her greetings and partings grew warmer, until both became consistently warm. She had gradually won a small victory over the demon.

Over the course of our visits, I've made it a point to bring Jocelyn her favorite homemade meals and treats from childhood, and her favorite childhood possessions, which I had intentionally saved for her. I also gave her copies of the cards, letters, and e-mails that I had sent to her over the years that we were alienated, in case they had been intercepted and not given to her. She seems to cherish these things. They are tangible proof that she was never forgotten, and that I had made many efforts to contact her, despite what she may have been told.

Jocelyn has come with me to attend a few family functions on my side of her family after being completely alienated from them for fifteen years. It was especially fortunate that she was able to reunite with her grandparents, as they are now in their eighties. Sadly, it seems likely that her brother will not be as fortunate.

Jocelyn still never calls me "Mom" verbally, though she does so in writing when she sends affectionate cards and notes for my birthday, Mother's Day, and holidays. During one of my earliest visits to her apartment, I noticed birthday cards on display. One of them was from her designated "surrogate mother," whom she has never mentioned to this day. The card read, "Once upon a time I wished upon a star for a daughter . . . and then you came." It confirmed what I had suspected, given my parental alienation research and my personal experience as an alienated parent—that my ex-husband had partnered with a woman who was happy to become his co-alienator in order to satisfy her own psychopathological needs at the expense of my children's need to maintain a relationship with their mother. Therefore, it appears that my daughter had not just one alienator, but at least three: her father, his partner, and her brother. And there may have been others. It had to take tremendous courage on her part to dare to have even a secret relationship with me and my family, given what she is up against.

I have a lot of respect for my daughter for being so brave. My wish is that my son, and every other alienated child, will eventually be able to find that same courage.

The parental alienation demon is so pervasive and tenacious that it gives the appearance of being impossible to exorcise. It was my love for my daughter that compelled me to go into battle against this daunting evil force in order to steal her back—not only for myself but also for herself. Every tiny bit of her that I was able to reclaim increased my fortitude to return to combat in order to reclaim still more of her. It remains a war in progress. And I would go right back to the battlefield, in a heartbeat, for my son.

Chapter Seven

Hope and Healing

After the painfully tragic and depressing stories in the earlier chapters in this book, the stories of reconciliation bring welcome respite and relief. These stories confirm that some alienated children and targeted parents find their way back to each other. In fact, the stories suggest that there are many different ways that this can happen, many paths from alienation to reconciliation. This was also found to be true in the stories of formerly alienated children, as Baker reports in *Adult Children of Parental Alienation Syndrome: Breaking the Ties that Bind.*[1]

CATALYSTS TO RECONCILIATION

Baker identifies eleven catalysts described by one or more of the forty adults she interviewed. These catalysts are presented in table 7.1, along with an explanation and examples—when applicable—found in the current stories.

In reading the reconciliation stories submitted for this book, it is far from clear which catalyst was most compelling or pressing for each child, especially because the stories are told from the perspective of the targeted parent and not the formerly alienated child. Moreover, there appear to be multiple catalysts at work for each child. For example, Gail's daughter probably reached maturity and for the first time experienced a physical separation from her father, and she reached her tolerance for being manipulated and abused by him.

The stories as told by the alienated children in Baker's book were far more complete narratives because the children had lived the experience of

Table 7.1.   Catalysts for Reconciliation

Catalyst	Explanation	Example
Maturation	The child has increasing number of opportunities to observe the ways that people in other families behave and begins to slowly question the story of his or her own family, especially as—in addition to life experience—the child has increased cognitive maturity and capacity to question his or her own upbringing and the capacity to tolerate psychological distance from his or her parents.	Gail's daughter went to college and for the first time was not under the immediate supervision and control of her father. Her daughter had opportunities to discuss her family situation with new college friends who had not been exposed to the vilification of her mother, which encouraged her to rethink her father's narrative.
Alienating Parent Turned on the Child	The favored parent becomes overly and unnecessarily controlling and harsh with the child, showing him-/herself to be the mean and vindictive person he or she really is.	Gail's daughter was subjected to her father's cruel and harsh treatment of her once he found out that she was spending time with her mother. This included trying to have her arrested for driving a car he had bought for her.
Experiencing Parental Alienation as a Parent	The grown alienated child marries an alienating parent and experiences parental alienation from the perspective of the targeted parent. That child comes to realize that his or her own childhood may have not been as it seemed.	This catalyst was not relevant for any of the stories submitted, as none of the alienated children had yet been married and divorced.
The Targeted Parent Returned	The child has the opportunity to experience the rejected parent due to enforcement of court orders, and in that process finds out that the rejected parent is not the monster he or she was made out to be.	Both Dan's and Seth's children experienced a reemergence of their rejected fathers due to the eventual enforcement of court-ordered parenting time. It seems likely that through the actual contact with the real person, the children were able to see the targeted parents for who they were.

Attaining a Milestone	Becoming a parent, graduating from college, getting married, and similar lifetime milestones create an emotional desire to reconnect with the targeted parent or create the impetus to reexamine the narrative from a new perspective.	It is possible that Claudia's daughter's admission into an advanced educational program was an impetus for her to reach out to her mother, although she presented the reason to her mother as a need for financial assistance.
Therapy	Discussions with a neutral and caring third party may lead to questioning the assumptions and the narrative from the family and can result in a desire to rethink the past and be open to a different future.	Several of the stories involved the alienated children attending therapy, although the extent to which the therapy played a role in creating the new understanding of the alienation and the targeted and favored parents is not clear.
Intervention of Extended Family Member	A trusted relative encourages the child to question and rethink his or her harsh stance toward the rejected parent.	This was not present in any of the stories submitted as far as can be determined.
Intervention of a Significant Other	An important and trusted significant other encourages the child to question and rethink his or her harsh stance toward the rejected parent.	One story submitted described how her friend's mother sat the alienated child down for a heart-to-heart talk and provided her with a different perspective on the child's parents. She encouraged the child to give her mother another chance, which soon led to a reconciliation. In another story the formerly alienated child recalled to her father that her boyfriend helped her to see things from a different perspective.
Seeing the Alienating Parent Mistreat Others	The child witnesses the alienating parent's harsh and cruel treatment of other people and comes to realize that the targeted parent may have been a victim in the family drama.	In one story, the alienated child recalled to her father once she reconciled with him that her mother (the alienating parent) had made many enemies in her life because she was not capable of treating people with kindness and respect. Eventually that helped to open the daughter's eyes to her mother's true nature and intentions.
Discovering That the Alienating Parent Was Dishonest	The alienated child has the opportunity to witness unambiguously dishonest behavior on the part of the favored parent, which creates a crack in the armor of that parent's supposed perfection.	This catalyst was not evident in any of the stories submitted for this book.

Becoming a Parent	Having one's own child allows the alienated child (as an adult) to realize the importance of both parents for the health and well-being of a child and question why the favored parent insisted on the child's rejection of the other parent.	This catalyst was not applicable to any of the stories submitted for this book, as none of the alienated children had children of their own.

making the decision to reconcile and could identify the triggers of reconciliation. In contrast, the stories as told by the targeted parents reflect the fact that, as an outsider, they did not really know for sure which influence was the most compelling for their children. Practically speaking, what this means is that targeted parents—while living the alienation and reconciliation drama—cannot necessarily know what will work for their particular child.

What is consistent across the two perspectives (stories told by the "adult children" and stories told by targeted parents) is that there are a number of different catalysts for reconciliation. This represents both good news and bad news. The bad news is that there doesn't yet seem to be a way to know which catalyst will work for which alienated child. The reconciliation process seems to unfold in a somewhat idiosyncratic and unpredictable manner. There is no (as of yet) known correspondence between a particular experience (for example, the targeted parent's fighting in court to reunify with the child) and a particular response (opening of the child's heart, rethinking his or her assumptions about the value of the targeted parent). The good news is that there are multiple pathways from alienation to reconciliation. This means, in theory at least, that there are numerous opportunities for something to take hold in the child, some vision of a different way to live, some feeling of dissatisfaction with the current state of affairs, some action that can create the opening for reconciliation to begin.

REASON FOR HOPE

These stories of reconciliation, more than anything else, offer hope. They confirm that someday, sometimes, alienated children can in fact find their way back to their targeted parent. Knowing that this is true is extremely helpful, if not essential, for currently targeted parents, as it provides them with the much-needed beacon of hope from which they can draw their strength to forge ahead in their own alienation battle. The hope of a better tomorrow fuels them each and every day and guides them on their journey. Without that hope, some may give up.

The stories of reconciliation also offer another kind of hope —one that is more immediate—and that is the hope that their children will benefit from their efforts to reconnect with them (the unanswered calls, the unreturned e-mails and text messages, the declined invitations) even while those same efforts are being denigrated and devalued.

When a parent attends a ceremony or sporting event uninvited and overtly unwanted, they do so with the belief that their children will feel loved seeing their face in the crowd. Usually there is no way in that moment to know with any certainty that what those parents are doing is actually awakening or connecting with their children. There is no recognizable sign that their showing up made a difference. More likely, the alienated child will show disdain for the targeted parent and make them feel unwelcome and uncomfortable (ignoring them, snubbing them, angrily asking why they even bothered to attend).

That is where the stories come into play. Hearing stories of reconciled children validates for currently targeted parents that their small but persistent efforts are not in vain. For example, when Seth heard that his daughter had been reading his e-mails all along, despite having never responded to them or acknowledged him in any way, he was reassured that he was in fact connecting with his children by continuing to reach out to them—that he was on the right path. Seth drew strength from the stories of others, and now his story will be an inspiration to future targeted parents who will maintain their efforts because of the strength they draw from his story. When Ava admitted to the therapist that she was reading his e-mails, it confirmed for Seth and for future targeted parents who hear this story that there is a reason to persevere.

LITTLE THINGS HAVE BIG MEANING

It is also hopeful that the efforts—big and small—of the targeted parent carry much more meaning than the alienated child is willing to let on at the time. Several of the parents wrote of sending care packages filled with little tokens of love and thought, and most, if not all, of the targeted parents mentioned continuing to send e-mail messages, text messages, and voice messages— despite rarely, if ever, receiving a response. Sometimes the targeted parents wondered if what they were doing made any difference, whether their efforts were "too little, too late," but they forged on, erring on the side of hope—the hope that their efforts would somehow be noticed or felt by their child.

WHAT THE TARGETED PARENTS DID RIGHT

Forge ahead they did. And in that process, they did a lot of things right, things that facilitated their children one day coming back to them. Five examples are highlighted below.

They Became Educated and Informed

In most of the stories submitted, the targeted parents wrote about how helpful it was to become educated and informed about the topic of parental aliena-tion. They scoured bookstores, trolled the Internet, joined support groups, and accepted their identity as a "targeted parent." Gail reported spending "nearly every waking minute" thinking about the problem and how to solve it. Dan wrote about how helpful it was to know that what he was dealing with had a name, and that he received a lot of good information about parental alienation from his attorney. Seth spoke of the inspiration he drew from Alec Baldwin's book, *A Promise to Ourselves*, knowing that if this tragedy could happen to a celebrity, then perhaps there was no shame in its happening to him. Others found inspiration in Baker's *Adult Children of Parental Aliena-tion Syndrome*, as the book confirms that the alienated children want a rela-tionship with the rejected parent despite not being able to admit it to the parent, the courts, mental health professionals, or even themselves. With this knowledge, they had the power of their convictions. Seth said that the take-away message in that book "stayed with me during my terrible ordeal and remains my mantra to this day."

Another aspect of targeted parents' becoming informed and educated is finding and retaining the right mental health and legal professionals to assist them. Many targeted parents wrote of seeking parental alienation experts and ensuring that whatever professional touched their lives understood what pa-rental alienation was and how it could negatively affect their children.

They Never Gave Up

The targeted parents heroically maintained their vigilance in pursuing their children, regardless of the pain and suffering it cost them. Each in their own way trudged on despite their exhaustion, despair, and sadness. They called their children knowing that the calls would be unanswered, they sent text messages that were never responded to, they sent e-mails that were blocked or unread. Dan reported, "I never went a day without trying to reach him by phone or text message." They showed up at graduations despite not having been invited, they paid tuition for schools they had not helped select, and they attended sporting events hoping to catch a glimpse of their children. They did this despite the experience being incredibly painful, knowing their children would most likely rebuff them, if not actually treat them with hostility. They did this knowing they would have to bear witness to the alienating parent in the coveted position of having easy access to the children and obvious influence over them. They did this because they never gave up.

They Saw the Alienation from the Child's Perspective

What helped the targeted parents stay focused despite the harsh and cold treatment of their alienated children toward them was their understanding that their children were suffering. They saw their children as victims rather than as perpetrators. Seeing the alienation experience from their child's perspective (rather than through the lens of their own pain and suffering) allowed them to maintain an empathic stance toward their children and provided these parents with the impetus to forge ahead.

The targeted parents understood that despite the callous behavior and claims of hatred and fear, their children very much needed and wanted them. This perspective made it possible for them to let go of their hurt and anger toward their children. They understood that this would have only entrenched the alienation further by confirming the poisonous messages the children were already receiving about them. The parents spoke of being heartbroken at how much their children suffered, how sad it must be for their children to forgo having a relationship with them.

Seth's therapist encouraged him to understand that his daughter was "torn between showing her true feelings and showing hatred toward me as she had been taught." A mother wrote that she attended conferences, ceremonies, and graduations for her children, "standing in the background quietly just to let them know that I was here," believing that it was important for her son to feel loved by her. In this sense, the targeted parents practiced what nationally renowned experimental and social psychologist Phillip Zimbardo refers to in his most recent book, *The Lucifer Effect*, as "dispositional charity," which requires understanding that the characteristics of the situation (the alienation dynamic) can elicit negative qualities in a person (the behaviors of the alienated child) that can mask or override their true nature.[2]

This dispositional charity created a place in the targeted parents' hearts to hold on to their love for their child and gave those parents the strength and reason to respond to their child with loving-kindness throughout the alienation and reconciliation process. We have no doubt that on some level, at least some of the time, the alienated children felt the love of their targeted parents and were drawn to its warmth and light as a much-needed antidote to the darkness of the abuse and manipulation of the alienating parent.

Seeing the alienation from the child's perspective involves what psychologist and English professor George Thompson and journalist Jerry Jenkins refer to as "verbal judo," which means engaging with people in a way that honors their position even when you don't agree with it: "If our opponent says something is black and we counter by insisting it is white, lines have been drawn for what will probably be an irresolvable conflict. If instead we move in the direction of our opponent by saying, 'I can see why you would say that is black,' we are neutralizing the thrust of our opponent and conserving our own energy. Most important we are maintaining a state of open-mindedness."[3] They point out the benefits of seeing a situation from the other person's perspective when trying to resolve a conflict: "Only then can you help the person see the consequences of what he is doing or is about to do. Only then can you help him make enlightened decisions."[4]

Some of the targeted parents appeared to practice the fine art of "verbal judo" when they interacted with their alienated children with love, respect, and empathy despite their own hurt feelings. This laid the foundation for a more loving and respectful relationship in the future.

They Respected the Child's Pace

Another important lesson from the stories is the need to understand that the process of reconciliation requires incredible care and patience. Reconciling with an alienated child is like caring for a delicate and fragile flower that needs tending to with just the right balance of all the essential ingredients. The targeted parents approached their alienated children as they would a frightened deer who could startle and skitter away at any moment. Slowly, ever so slowly, the targeted parents approached their alienated children, mindful of keeping their own expectations at bay, keeping their attention focused on the signals and signs from their children.

This dance of rapprochement required an exquisite attunement to the child's need to control the pace of the reconciliation. Once again the parents needed to put their children's needs above their own, understanding that their children would reconcile in their own way and at their own speed. To force the reunification process would be disrespectful and could put at risk the enterprise of reestablishing a loving bond with their lost child. Claudia's description of her daughter cautiously circling around her, moving slowly closer as trust was developed, provides an excellent illustration of this dance and the patience required of targeted parents.

They Didn't Expect an Apology

When we are hurt by someone we love, most of us want some form of acknowledgement and an apology to make things right again. We want the other person to understand that we are hurt and that it was their behavior that was hurtful to us. We desire a shared understanding, and it is through that shared understanding that we can forge forgiveness. Hurt feelings can be soothed by the other person's compassion for our suffering and assurance that we will not be hurt again. It is human to want and expect an apology and to desire the opportunity to forgive the other person. This exchange allows for healing to take place. Identifying the elements of this exchange is the focus of many self-help books on broken relationships. For example, psychologist David J. Lieberman describes nine steps for repairing a broken relationship, such as talking it through, showing appreciation for the other person, and the like.[5]

However, these kinds of steps are typically not possible when it comes to alienation. When an alienated child reconciles with his targeted parent, there often is no such forging of a shared understanding, mostly because the child is still a child and the targeted parent understands that it is not appropriate to expect a child to articulate a full accounting of the ways in which the alienation caused pain to the parent. Moreover, because reconciliation is a process, at the beginning of which the child is still partially alienated, the child is in no frame of mind to contritely ask for the targeted parent's forgiveness. A further complicating factor is that while the child has in fact caused considerable pain to the targeted parent through his or her words and actions, it was at the behest of and under the influence of someone else (the alienating parent), and so an apology may not feel appropriate or necessary to either the child or the parent.

In the stories submitted for this book, the reconciliation of the broken relationship between the child and the targeted parent occurred despite the absence of most, if not all, of the markers of reconciliation, such as a full accounting of what was wrong, contrition, apology, and forgiveness. The targeted parents who understood that these elements were not possible or appropriate fared better than those who did not. In one story, for example, the father reported "forgiving" his formerly alienated daughter only to struggle with his own feelings of anger and resentment toward her. These feelings became manifest in their relationship and ultimately led to another breach between them.

Most targeted parents seemed to understand and accept that their children were victims and therefore were not responsible for their actions, no matter how painful those actions were for them.

CONCLUSION

There are many catalysts to alienated children reconciling with their targeted parent. Some stories seemed to involve more than one catalyst, and it was not always clear from the stories which catalysts were at work for which children. Nonetheless, the stories unequivocally confirm that some alienated children come back to their lost parents, and that when they do, it is possible to forge a close and loving bond where before there was only distance and pain.

While waiting for their alienated children to come back to them, the targeted parents engaged in many productive behaviors, including becoming informed and educated, never giving up on their children, viewing the alienation from their child's perspective, accepting that the pace of the reconciliation would be set by the child, and not expecting an apology. Together, these actions and attitudes gave them hope, helped them set their sights on their long-term goal, and helped them maintain their love for the children, no matter what.

Part IV

Moving Forward

Chapter Eight

Living with Alienation

The targeted parents reported experiencing a range of emotions throughout their unfolding alienation drama and—for those fortunate enough to reunite with their child—over the course of reconciliation. This chapter will explore the emotions that accompany parental alienation and provide concrete suggestions to targeted parents for coping and living within the vortex of the alienation drama, both as it unfolds and as it resolves itself.

THE EMOTIONAL LIFE OF A TARGETED PARENT

Most of targeted parents' emotions were negative, with alienation described by the parents who submitted their stories as "my biggest nightmare," the "worst experience of my life," and "a harrowing ordeal that never really ends."

Sadness, Loss, and Yearning

The principal feeling for targeted parents was one of sadness, loss, and yearning for their absent children. The separation from their children, for the targeted parent, was agonizing. One man returned home to find his wife and children "simply gone," and another said that he was "beside myself" when he couldn't be around his children. Many parents spoke of the loss in physical terms, as if a part of their body—or their whole being—was wounded, such as the mother who wrote, "I felt my heart being torn from my chest."

Unlike other kinds of loss, the yearning for the alienated child did not dissipate with time. Nora said, "Not a day goes by that I don't think of them and have a lump in my throat. . . . I miss my sons with every ounce of my being. I miss the children that they once were. I feel I was robbed of their childhood and robbed of my motherhood. . . . [T]he tears are always just behind my eyes." For these parents, there is no separation from the experience of loss. Even the most mundane tasks, such as going to the grocery store, can trigger sadness and longing for the absent children.

Unending Suffering

As many targeted parents have commented, short of death, losing a child to parental alienation may be the hardest thing a parent has to contend with. Dan described it as "something huge and hard" being lodged in his chest. In some ways, it might have been more difficult than a death because there was no easy way to explain to other people what was happening. The wellspring of support and comfort that typically surrounds a parent who has lost a child to death was noticeably absent for these targeted parents. Moreover, unlike a death, there was no natural progression through the stages of grief as described in Elizabeth Kübler-Ross's seminal work, *On Death and Dying.*[1] There was no closure and each day brought with it the possibility of new insult, injury, and pain (another allegation, another court motion, another milestone to be excluded from).

Being a targeted parent required living with an open wound that for many resulted in a feeling of numbness, with the pain and sadness seeping into all of the corners of their life, making it nearly impossible to find any solace or pleasure. Knowing their child was "out there" in the world—growing, learning, changing, developing—represented a kind of slow torture, the way that a starved person pressing his or her nose against the bakery window feels even more hungry upon smelling the freshly baked bread. These targeted parents were starving for their children, with the hunger pangs worsening with each passing day.

Even those who reconciled had to live with the knowledge that there was no way to make up for the lost time—for them or for their children. There was an irreparable tear, a hole in the fabric of their lives.

Concern for Their Child

Adding to the pain and suffering was the knowledge that their alienated children were being warped and harmed by the alienating parents and they, the targeted parents, were unable to protect them.

One father wrote of how gut-wrenching it was to see the effects on his daughter while she was being overmedicated to enforce her compliance with the alienation: "Once again my daughter became lethargic and unemotional. She would carry her baggie full of pills with her when she came for her visitation. It broke my heart." Another man, who had witnessed his stepdaughter being alienated from her father, realized only too well what his own children were being put through: "It broke my heart to see them starting to go through the same things that their older sister had gone through." Dan experienced his son testifying in court against him and ached for him: "I knew how I felt, how hard this day was. I couldn't even imagine how difficult this must be for him." Anna's heart ached for her little girl who was being manipulated to forgo communication with her during separations and told that her mother was stealing her money: "I felt so sad for my little girl who was being given the message that she was not allowed to miss her mommy. . . . This was one of the saddest things I had ever experienced, and so totally unnecessary."

Even the parents who eventually reconciled with their alienated children had to live with the knowledge that they had not been able to shield their children from the alienation and its effects. Gail expressed, "I am thankful each day that I got my daughter back, although saddened by what he put her through." Most parents feel a primal—almost physical—need to protect their children, and targeted parents, unable to do so due to circumstances beyond their control, felt unbearable pain.

Shock and Awe

The language of war was prevalent throughout the stories of alienation. Many targeted parents spoke of alienation as a war that they had been drafted into for the heart and mind of their child. They wrote of the alienating parent as a determined opponent who respected no rules of engagement, was unwilling to compromise or negotiate on any terms, and spared no expense to win at all costs. Anna described her ex-husband as "my own personal terrorist. I never knew what trouble he would inflict on me and in what way he would intrude into my life." There were periods of calm, and then, seemingly out of the blue, another attack would be launched, another motion filed, another parenting time interfered with, another opportunity for the child to love and be loved missed.

In the war of alienation, the targeted parent was an unwilling combatant and for that reason was often caught off guard. Targeted parents wrote of being unprepared and continually surprised at the lengths to which their

former spouse would go, shocked by the viciousness, cruelty, and maliciousness of their maneuvers. Joe realized that his wife had been scheming behind
his back for years in order to bankrupt him. In one fell swoop he found out
that he didn't really know who his wife was or what she was capable of doing
to him. "This was all happening so quickly that I could not begin to process
how my life was being destroyed."

For someone who doesn't think the way an alienator thinks, it can be
quite shocking to realize that the other person does not have the same values
or moral constraints as themselves. The targeted parent had assumed that
everyone was working from the same set of rules and then found out quite
suddenly that the other person was operating under an entirely different set of
rules than they were. The most shocking aspect seemed to be that the actions
of the alienating parent—while presented as being in the best interests of the
child—were obviously harmful, if not actually abusive. This parent who was
claiming to love the child was behaving in a manner that was highly likely to
result in the child being unnecessarily hurt. Punishing the targeted parent and
having the child all to themselves seemed to be the ultimate goal of the
alienating parent, and the eventual erosion of the child's well-being was
merely collateral damage.

Adding to the shock was the speed with which the relationship progressed
from being between unhappy marital partners to being mortal enemies. One
woman was led to believe that she and her husband would calmly sit down
and explain to the children that the marriage was ending, only to find that her
soon-to-be-ex-husband had entirely different plans: "I was blindsided and in
total shock as my husband suddenly turned on an Oscar-worthy performance
in front of the children." Rather than explaining that he had been having an
affair and wanted to end the marriage, he sobbed to the children that their
mother didn't love him anymore. She had not seen it coming and was at
a significant disadvantage from that point forward. Her ex-husband had
created the narrative that formed the template of the children's understanding
of the divorce.

Seth, too, was caught off guard: "When this all started, I was in shock,
could not sleep well, and became depressed." It was disorienting to realize
that little was as it seemed, and that one's trust had been misplaced and one's
assumptions and plans were grossly misguided.

The coldness of and rejection by their children also shocked the targeted
parents. Anna's daughter referred to her as cheap following a shopping spree
for a new wardrobe; Seth was called a loser by his children; and Nora's

children believed that she was so incompetent as to be incapable of operating the home's thermostat or assisting with their middle school homework. Seth's daughter, even after months of positive weekend visits, filed criminal charges against him that resulted in his being jailed. He reported feeling "flabbergasted" when that happened. It is as if each maneuver made by their ex or their children constantly caught the targeted parents off guard and unprepared. One parent wrote, "I was surprised at how flippant she was about it. . . . Kathy didn't see anything wrong with listing Dave as their father instead of me." The targeted parents came to realize that they no longer had a shared reality with their ex and that they could not assume even the most basic courtesy or respect from the other parent of their child.

Desperate

Another common feeling reported by these targeted parents was that of desperation. They were desperate for knowledge, desperate to reconnect with their lost child, and desperate to stop the train wreck of alienation from crashing through their lives. They wrote, "I was desperately in need of help and had nowhere to turn," and "I was naïve and desperate. I spent the next ten months trying to beg, plead, and reason with my ex-husband to return Callie to me." Nora wrote that she was "[h]eartbroken and searching for solutions and answers." The targeted parents were in pain, and more than anything, they desperately wanted the pain to end and for the nightmare to be over.

Like war veterans, these targeted parents probably suffered from a form of post-traumatic stress disorder (PTSD)—shell-shocked from their terrible ordeal of slow-motion loss and rejection. This may account for the experience of loss of affect that some parents described, a feeling of flatness and disengagement from their everyday life. As Gail poignantly described in her story, "The loss of my daughter cast a shadow over my life. It dulled the taste of the most delicious food. . . . Some days I felt like a zombie, the walking dead. . . . The dull ache was . . . like the beating of my heart."

Many parents wrote of the difficulty of compartmentalizing their pain in order to prevent it from pervading their lives. It was like an open wound, crying out for attention, that they carried with them wherever they went.

Weary

The stories of alienation are stories of battle-weary parents suffering for years on end. For them, alienation was a long and slow process—a long process for their child to become alienated and a long process for their child to come back to them. Many of the parents who wrote their stories had been alienated from their children for several years. In the life experience of these children and parents, this was not a short-term blip, something that they would one day look back on and wonder how they ever could have gotten so worried and worked up. This was a fork in the road that led the family down an entirely different path from one that anyone could have anticipated. No one could have wanted this new path. This was a way of life, not a minor detour.

One targeted parent wrote, "I realized later it was only the beginning of a long difficult journey, a journey through parental alienation syndrome's horrific trials and tribulations." Because the alienation followed the marriage's dissolution, which itself was painful, stressful, and distressing, the parents were already stressed and strained emotionally and financially. One parent explained, "I thought my divorce was awful but the real drama began after my divorce was final." And Nora commented, "It has been eight years since I last saw or heard from my two sons. It is as unbelievable to me today as it was when I first lost them."

Worried and Afraid

Worrying about how much worse things could get appeared as a common refrain throughout the stories. Targeted parents made statements such as "I feared that all was lost," "I feared that I would lose them forever," and "I feared that I would never hear from her again." Anna went to bed each night wondering how many more attacks on their relationship she and her daughter could withstand. She also wrote of dreading the mail delivery each day, "never knowing what new packet of lies and deception would be waiting for me."

This kind of hypervigilance to environmental cues is consistent with PTSD, in which the smallest sight, smell, and sound can trigger a trauma response of fear and worry, like the returned warrior who senses snipers and landmines within the suburban landscape. Dan, too, reported that he was "always waiting for that other shoe to drop."

These parents had no peace, for even in quiet times, they knew that their former spouse was working diligently to undermine their relationship with their children and to wreak havoc and cause pain in their lives. When things did take a turn for the worse, they wrote, "My worst fears were borne out," as if they had been anticipating this outcome all along.

In fact, targeted parents had a lot to worry about. They worried about the progression of the alienation, they worried about their finances, but most of all they worried about the negative impact of the alienation on the character and well-being of their children. They were all too aware of the fact that their children who to outsiders might appear to be cherished and prized—were actually being poorly parented, if not actually mistreated, by the alienating parent.

The targeted parents were also worried that their own compromised parenting would affect their children. They realized that they could not parent in the way that they wanted to because their authority had been eroded and devalued. They couldn't effectively set limits and teach their children respect without risking allegations of abuse and instigating conflict with their children.

Choosing to maintain the relationship above all else, targeted parents were keenly aware that their fear of the risk of allegations of abuse and of instigating conflict with their children also could create problems for the children later in life. Dan tiptoed around his daughter following the alienation of his son, doing whatever he could to prevent her from leaving him as well, even though that meant that he could not really parent her the way he believed that she needed to be parented. He said, "I worried about what this would do to her in the long run but I was desperate not to lose her." And Gail, even after reconciling with her daughter, feared that their relationship might be taken away again. As a result, Gail was extremely cautious about how she approached her daughter: "I was worried about whether she would return to her father's for the summer and I wouldn't see her, but I was afraid of bringing up the subject." Gail didn't even feel comfortable enough to simply ask her daughter a question about her plans, so fearful was she of annoying her or turning her off.

Confused, Without a Plan of Action

As noted above, the targeted parents were in a war for the heart and mind of their child, but they lacked a coherent and articulated battle plan. They were on a journey, a path that was being created with each footstep, but there was no map to follow. No one could tell them what to do to make the pain stop, to end the nightmare, to get their children back. Thankfully, many found information on the Internet, and many targeted parents spoke of the importance of becoming educated and arming themselves with knowledge from books and experts. To know that what they were dealing with had a name was a source of great relief. Unfortunately, no book or expert could tell them exactly what to do in their particular situation, because the field was still evolving, especially at the time these stories took place.

Dan wrote, "I left his [the psychologist's] office armed with a lot of good information but no clear idea about how I could use it to prevent what was happening." Seth, for example, faced several decision points during his journey, forks in the road where he simply did not know what the right thing to do was: "At the time, I wondered whether this was the right move" and "I had my doubts as to what the right move was." And even after reconciling with her daughter, Claudia "silently wondered whether I was being a hero or an enabler."

Each day brought with it a new dilemma for the targeted parents. Should they proceed with their current plan or would that backfire? Should they be more proactive or should they back off? Will there be unintended consequences of their choices and actions? There was simply no way to know whether their choices in the end would be good ones. Living with that level of uncertainty brought with it tremendous additional stress for the battle-weary targeted parents.

Victimized by the System

Targeted parents were aware of the fact that it was the alienating parent who was creating the problem and causing their pain. Second in line for blame, however, was the family court system, with its incompetent, unprepared, uninformed, and uncaring mental health and legal professionals who financially benefited from the alienation and who could have helped but did not. Therefore, in addition to feeling victimized by the alienating parent, the targeted parents felt themselves to be victimized by the various social service and legal systems that their family came into contact with. They learned that a system that is biased toward protecting women and children (child protection, domestic relations) can be exploited by alienating parents.

Joe learned that "in cases of domestic violence, a man is usually guilty until proven innocent. I also learned that in order to prove my innocence, I would need time and a lot of money, neither of which I had." Another father shared, "Even though I had done nothing—there hadn't even been an argument—I was handcuffed and marched into a squad car. I was taken to a holding cell where I was taunted and harangued." Mothers, too, felt betrayed, devalued, and scarred by their interactions with the police, the courts, and child protection. Many targeted parents reported feeling outrage and shock at the apparent lack of kindness and competence they encountered, which only added to their overall level of pain and suffering.

Alone

Despite being in the fight of their lives, many targeted parents reported feeling alone and misunderstood by their friends and family. Gail tried in vain to find somebody—therapist, high school guidance counselor, parent of her child's friend—to advocate for her. No one did. Anna found that her friends and family could not really grasp what she was going through and gave her simplistic and unhelpful advice: "Throughout these years I was continually told by my friends and family to stop obsessing about what George was doing because I was giving him too much power to make my life miserable."

Not only were friends and family unhelpful, but so were many mental health professionals who sided with the children and could not see past those children's campaigns of denigration, borrowed scenarios, and other behavioral manifestations to recognize the alienation for what it was. Many targeted parents felt betrayed, misunderstood, and alone in their ordeal. Nora shared, "At one point a family specialist was assigned to our case. I have never felt more betrayed or outraged in my life. . . . This was true of others as well. The more I tried to tell my side of the story, the more everyone disbelieved me." Joe wrote of attending school conferences only to see the "expression of pure hatred [that] crossed the faces of the teachers." And because his ex-wife led them to believe that he was an abusive parent, another father had to contend with the "complete and total disrespect" of nurses tending to his dying father.

Anger and Frustration

Targeted parents also wrote about feeling angry at the underhanded and harmful schemes of the alienating parent. For example, several parents wrote about feeling angry when their children were taken to psychiatrists and put on medications that were not deemed necessary. They believed that the behavior and treatment of the professionals was unethical and improper and allowed the alienating parent to effectively control the physical and emotional life of the child. Other parents were angry when they felt displaced and replaced by a new partner or spouse of the alienating parent: "I was furious. I asked her not to have the kids call Dave 'Daddy Dave.'"

Some parents felt chronic frustration at the interference of the other parent: "It was also very frustrating when the kids abruptly ended our brief conversations because their stepfather wanted them to do the dishes." Another father was told his child couldn't come to the phone because the child was playing with the cat, as if that were more important than a connection with his other parent. There was a lot to be angry about as a targeted parent, including the lies and deception of the other parent, the waste of family resources on unnecessary legal maneuvers, the unnecessary pain inflicted on the children, and the lost time between parent and child.

Energized/Committed/Focused/Courageous

A range of negative emotions flooded targeted parents on a daily basis, enlisting them in a war they did not want and were not prepared to fight. Nonetheless, they managed to cope and draw on an unwavering commitment to their children during the long and arduous journey. They experienced themselves as being on a mission to rescue their children and this mission infused their lives with purpose and meaning. They developed identities as targeted parents fighting for their children. Seth said, "What helped me is that I am a very persistent person with a lot of fight in me." Gail wrote, "I spent nearly every waking minute thinking about how to rescue my daughter," while Joe said he "launched into the fight of my life."

These parents understood that they were in a war and realized that they needed to marshal their resources and develop a plan of engagement. For Gail, that meant calling her daughter every day regardless of the pain it caused her—"no matter how painful it was, no matter how sad I felt, no matter how devastating it was to hear her voice message." Gail was able to put her feelings of sadness aside in order to enact her plan. Just setting out the plan allowed her to do the right thing without having to think about it. She didn't have to figure out if she was going to call, or determine whether she was up for making the call, or think through whether it was the right thing to do. She had made her plan and she stuck with it because she didn't have to think it through each day. Doing so might have led to her skipping days or forgoing it all together. Essentially, she put the plan into motion and it became automatic. She left her office, headed for the subway, and placed the call.

What seemed to motivate these parents throughout was the belief that their children needed them. Fighting for their children allowed them to feel like a parent again: "Despite the hardships I encountered, I never considered giving up, as I believed with all of my heart that one day my daughter would thank me."

Throughout this war that they did not want to fight, they learned that they had inner reserves they never knew they had: "It would be my own personal journey as well, discovering my frailties as a human being and my untapped strength to work through those weaknesses to find a strength I never knew I had." They learned something about themselves: that they had strength, courage, and fortitude when it counted the most. Claudia wrote that despite being war weary, she would never stop fighting for her children: "It remains a war in progress. And I would go right back to the battlefield, in a heartbeat, for my son."

Patient

The targeted parents who got their children back, and those still waiting for that to happen, needed to summon vast reserves of patience in the face of excruciating suffering and unfulfilled yearning for their lost children. These parents understood that, to a great extent, there were many external forces at work over which they had little control, including the concerted efforts of the alienating parent and his or her supporters; the slow, imprecise, and sometimes corrupt family court system; cautious and incompetent mental health professionals; and the unique personality and temperament of their child.

They learned that the only way to survive was to take the long view. It was essential for them to learn how to manage their frustration and intense feelings of yearning. Otherwise, they might be tempted to give in, give up, or make hasty decisions that could backfire and entrench the alienation even more. Dan exercised enormous patience while waiting for his ex-wife to eventually reveal herself to the courts: "She was a master manipulator, but I was patient. I believed that if she were given enough rope, she would eventually hang herself."

These parents told of waiting not months, but years, for a court date or for the judge to finally see the alienating parent's true colors. Only after observing that parent's repeated failures to comply with court orders would the judge be confident that the alienator was actually working against reconciliation despite crocodile tears and false claims of wanting the children to have a relationship with the other parent.

Time was the enemy of the targeted parent, as each passing day was forever lost, but time was also the savior, for it held the promise of the alienating parent's true intentions being revealed.

Patience was also required when dealing with the reconciliation process. The targeted parents were keenly aware that their children were most likely not going to come around all at once—that they would reopen their hearts in a careful and cautious manner, with one step closer and one step further away, fearful of getting hurt. The children needed to test the reality of their experience with the parent against the lies and distortions implanted by the alienating parent. In this dance of reconciliation, the children had the power to disappear again and the power to keep their hearts closed, and so the targeted parent had to exercise patience and permit the children to redevelop a sense of trust and security on their own time.

The parents needed to tame the tiger of their impatience to have their child back, to have a shared reality, to be able to rest assured that their child would not disappear again. They learned the necessity of being patient while allowing their children to set the pace of reconciliation. As Claudia commented, "So I have learned that the progress of renewing our relationship must be gauged by her pace, and not according to my or anyone else's timeline. . . . All in all, it has been a painfully slow process."

Careful

Part of being patient also involved being careful not to ask for too much, not to push too hard, not to be too intense, and not to show their needs. As Gail noted, inside she was screaming, but outside she was calm, cool, and collected. She was careful not to overwhelm her child with questions, demands, or emotions for fear of scaring her away. Dan "had to be polite and precise in everything I did. I walked on eggshells, as I feared that even normal parental discipline could be misunderstood by my ex-wife or serve as ammunition for her to accuse me of abuse." He couldn't parent his child as he wanted to for fear of antagonizing his ex-wife, worried that he would do something that could be used against him. Claudia wrote of how careful she was to maintain her boundaries, respect her daughter's need to set the pace, and not upset the "demon" of the alienation.

The targeted parents also had to be careful to protect themselves from getting hurt or disappointed by their child again. This was especially true for the parents who had begun the reconciliation process. They had lived for, dreamed of, and desired reconciliation with every ounce of their being for so many years that when it finally began to look like a reality, they had to steel themselves against what could be a devastating disappointment if it didn't come to pass. Moreover, they came to realize that their alienated child was not the person she or he once had been; their child had grown and changed in the process, and was in some respects a stranger. Claudia in particular was wary of her daughter's attempts to reconcile and asked herself, "Is my daughter looking to rekindle our relationship or is she just looking for another money tree?"

Grateful

The primary emotional reaction of targeted parents to the reconciliation process was absolute gratitude for every single second with their child. Even mundane tasks were infused with magic and wonder. Dan commented, "Having him with me, doing an ordinary task, brought me to tears." Seth wrote, "I felt like a real father again, doing car pools and sharing a moment/memory with one of my daughters and her friends."

For some, when the dream became a reality after all of the struggle and sacrifice, reconciliation seemed almost too good to be true. Keenly aware of so many other targeted parents who had not yet reconciled, these parents felt eternally grateful to have this opportunity to once again be a parent to their child. They felt that they would never take their children for granted. Gail said, "I am thankful each day that I got my daughter back," and Seth wrote, "I feel like a parent again even though I was robbed of years of true, loving fatherhood."

The memory of the pain is never forgotten and tinges the pleasure with a bittersweet essence of the awareness of how they almost lost their children for good. For Claudia, who was only partially reconciled, even the little bits that she had were extremely potent for her: "I cherish these windows of opportunity to have 'my girl' back. . . . For now, these crumbs of a relationship are a welcome relief from the starvation of having been completely alienated from her for so many years." The times that she does have with her daughter allow her to regain her identity as a mother. They energize her to forge on and even entertain the idea of going into battle again, if necessary, to rescue her son from the grip of alienation.

LIVING WITH ALIENATION

Based on the lessons learned from the targeted parents who have written their stories for this book, the following nine suggestions are offered to help targeted parents cope and live with their alienation experience. We are writing this section directly to you, the targeted parent, with the hope that the suggestions can be immediately useful and practical for you.

Conceptualize Alienation as a Battle

Alienation is a battle for the heart and mind of your child. As a targeted parent, you need to steel yourself for the prospect of a prolonged and protracted battle. Inner and external resources need to be reserved and allocated as necessary. You also need to expect the unexpected and not waste any time or energy being surprised or outraged at the behaviors of your ex. Accept that the life of a targeted parent will be filled with gross injustices, rude awakenings, and an enormous waste of time and money.

Because it is a battle, it is essential that you have a battle plan, a vision of what success would mean for you and your child, whether it is to hold on to the relationship before your child becomes more severely alienated or to reconcile with a currently alienated child. Once the goal is conceptualized, you can develop an action plan. The plan will help you stay focused and committed during times when you might despair and feel like giving up. The plan will help you see that each small step you take (each phone call, each letter, each option considered) is part of an overall strategy to one day get your child back. Part of the plan must involve taking the long view, understanding that the plan is long-term and not likely to result in immediate reconciliation or improvement or judicial action. Keeping expectations appropriately low and long-term can help buffer you from the crushing disappointment of failed efforts or lack of immediate results or timely action.

Exercise 8.1: Identifying Goals and Action Steps

In the space below, write down your primary goals with respect to your relationship with your child for the next month (e.g., have one phone call with your child), six months (e.g., increase parenting time), one year (e.g., have legal custody reinstated), and five years (e.g., be fully reconciled). Once you have identified your goals, think about what action steps are required in order to achieve them (e.g., identify and retain a new attorney, receive parenting coaching, find the necessary experts).

	Goals	*Action Steps*
Goal for Next Month:		
Goal for Next Six Months:		
Goal for Next Year:		
Goal for Five Years:		

Appreciate the Good

Some targeted parents can become consumed with the negative aspects of the experience and fail (or feel too guilty) to notice what is good and right in their lives. Yet there will be good times throughout the process, either with your child or in other areas of your life. It is essential for you as a targeted parent to be able to take pleasure where you can, and to take in and be present and awake to the pleasures that do exist. As a sufferer from chronic pain commented, "Pain and loss are not incompatible with joy and loving life."[2] There is no rule that says that a targeted parent should or must be miserable every second of every day. There is no need to feel ashamed or guilty for enjoying a good movie, having a laugh with a friend, or forgetting the alienation drama for a while. In fact, it will help you feel more energized for the next battle.

The best way to achieve this is through living a mindful life, being emotionally present to the moment-by-moment experiences that life has to offer. It may help to develop a meditation practice and develop an "attitude of gratitude" for what is good and what is working—even in the face of enormous struggle and suffering.

Exercise 8.2: Identifying What Is Good in Life

In the space below, write down some positive aspects of your life as it is being lived right now, even while the alienation is present. Consider positive aspects of each of the domains listed below. If there isn't currently anything positive in a particular domain, consider ways to change that.

	Positive Aspects	*Ways to Improve*
Health:		
Finances:		
Family of Origin:		
Work:		
Home:		
Significant Other:		
Hobbies:		

Take Care of Yourself

Targeted parents dealing with the enormous stress and strain of alienation may forget to take care of themselves. As a targeted parent, you may not be nurturing yourself in ways that will allow you to sustain the inner resources that you will need to call upon. You may forget to eat properly, get enough sleep, or exercise. You may neglect to monitor your physical and emotional health. It is essential that you keep an eye on yourself in order to manage your stress and find ways to cope with and heal from the alienation drama.

Meditation, for example, can provide helpful self-soothing and self-care opportunities, which are essential for you as a battle-weary targeted parent. Meditation can bring clarity and focus to the inner self and help you refrain from engaging in catastrophizing language that creates unnecessary fear and anxiety, so that you avoid living scenarios in your head that will never come to pass. Meditation can help you keep focused on what is most important, and not waste time and energy on things that don't really matter.

Self-care also involves checking in with yourself to see how things are going and what feelings are present. You can conduct these routine "check-ins" with yourself to see if more or different self-care is needed. Perhaps you need more social support, or more down time, or more distractions, or more sleep, or to eat better, or to exercise more. You must not forget to take care of yourself so that you can stay strong for the battle and so that you can be the best possible parent for your child to come home to.

In the same vein, you can work on any self-improvement projects that need attention. No one is perfect, and most likely you have areas of self-growth that you could work on (assertiveness, eating healthier, yoga, self-expression) to keep a positive momentum in your life.

Exercise 8.3: Self-Care

In the space below, write down ways in which you currently take care of yourself. For example, under "Exercise," you might list nothing in the "Currently" column, but in the "Future" column you might list that you plan to start taking a yoga class. Under "Food," you might indicate that you binge on sweets currently, but you plan to cut back in the near future.

	Currently	*Future*
Exercise:		
Food:		
Friendship/ Socializing:		
Sleeping:		
Hobbies:		
Significant Other:		
Other:		

Get Social Support

Targeted parents understandably crave validation and understanding from other people who have also experienced alienation. Too often the friends and family of targeted parents do not grasp the maliciousness of the alienating parent, the pain of being rejected by one's child, or the legitimacy of the fear that the child will eventually be gone from their life. They may also suffer from compassion fatigue. Targeted parents experience insult added to injury when their friends and family fail to empathically support them in their alienation journey. For this reason, targeted parents can benefit from spending time with other parents who have also experienced parental alienation. In that setting they can feel safe to share their worst fears, to despair, to express their most ugly and unacceptable thoughts and feelings because they can trust that the other parents truly appreciate where they are coming from.

Social worker and parental alienation expert Karen Lebow has written about the importance of social support for targeted parents in particular in "Supporting Targeted Parents."[3] We echo her sentiments and encourage you, as a targeted parent, to find a mutual social support group, ideally one that is run by a licensed mental health professional who can create a safe setting for you to share your grief and gain comfort and solace from those who are walking down the same road as you.

Exercise 8.4: Finding the Social Support You Need

So that you can systematically find one that works for you, in the space below, start to keep a list of avenues you have explored to identify a social support group.

Approach 1: Look on the Internet, such as on craigslist.org or meet-up.com, for notices for social support groups.
    Results so far:

Approach 2: E-mail experts in the field asking whether they know of any social support groups in your area.
    Results so far:

Approach 3: Look in the local paper under listings of social support groups to see if there is one for divorced parents that might address parental alienation issues.
    Results so far:

Other Approaches:

Find a Mental Health Provider Who Understands

In addition to the mutual support from a social support group, many targeted parents can benefit from the training, insight, and assistance of a licensed mental health professional, especially when that person truly understands the parental alienation dynamic. Therapists William and Lorna Goldberg identify the many potential benefits of individual psychotherapy for targeted parents, including helping them process their strong and sometimes overwhelming feelings, strengthening coping strategies, redefining expectations and accomplishments, and developing strategies for living with alienation.[4] We encourage you to explore the potential for psychotherapy to benefit you in your life.

Exercise 8.5: Consider Psychotherapy

In the space below, write down ways in which you think you could benefit from psychotherapy and ways in which you think you could experience any potential drawbacks. Rate each one on a five-point scale, with 0 = not at all, 1 = a little, 2 = somewhat, 3 = much, 4 = very much.

Rate the Potential Benefits

Help with Processing Emotions:
Help Strengthening Coping Skills:
Help Redefining Expectations:
Help Living with Alienation:
Others:

Rate Potential Drawbacks

Costs:
Time:
Creates Appearance of Weakness to Child or Courts:
Others:

Find Serenity

Regardless of whether you believe in a higher power, the serenity prayer can be a helpful reminder that there are only some things in life any of us have control over and that is what we should focus on. The original serenity prayer attributed to Rheinhold Niebur runs as follows:

> God, grant me the serenity to accept the things I cannot change,
> The courage to change the things I can,
> And wisdom to know the difference.

If you prefer a secular version, you can change the prayer to make it consistent with your belief system. For example, you could say:

> I strive to accept the things I cannot change,
> to find the courage to change the things I can,
> And to have the wisdom to know the difference.

Regardless of the specific words, the point of the prayer is to keep you focused on the fact that the person you have the most control over (some would say the only person you have any control over) is yourself. By acknowledging that you cannot change the alienating parent (and possibly your child as well, under these conditions), you free up the mental, emotional, and physical energy expended on trying to do so and you can channel your energy toward self-improvement, coping, and healing yourself. Acceptance of things that cannot be changed doesn't have to mean being "okay" with the alienation. Here, acceptance means seeing things for what they are and accepting the real-life limits and constraints you must currently contend with.

Exercise 8.6: Try Using or Creating a Serenity Prayer

Take the time to consciously and deliberately consider different serenity prayers until you find one that works for you. Consider printing or writing it on beautiful paper and posting it around your house so that you are face to face with it several times each day. Find ways to make it your own.

Develop a Mantra

There are many days when targeted parents don't see the point of continuing the battle and consider giving up. They see no results from their plan and have lost hope of ever reconciling with their lost children. The pain, humiliation, and frustration are simply too much. If you have times like these, it might be helpful to have a mantra, a saying that you can repeat to yourself that gives you the focus, energy, and drive necessary to forge on. For many targeted parents the mantra that seems to help is simply "My child needs me. I will never give up." This is a simple message that carries with it a huge potential for motivating even the most despairing targeted parent. By saying it you can remind yourself that your children need you, your children want you, and your children deserve you. When you say this mantra (or one like it), you can help yourself to hear your children calling for you to not give up on them, to put them first, to selflessly carry on because you are needed.

Exercise 8.7: Develop a Mantra

Take the time to consciously and deliberately consider different mantras until you find one that works for you. Consider typing it or writing it by hand on beautiful paper and posting it around your house so that you are face to face with it several times each day. Find ways to make it your own.

Call On a Helpful Image

Some targeted parents have also found it helpful to identify a guiding image or metaphor to refer to when they feel consumed with anger or hurt at the behavior and rejection of their child. The image or metaphor can help remind them that their child is a victim, not an abuser. For Claudia, it was the image that a demon had possessed her child. Any time her daughter did something she didn't like, Claudia conceptualized it as the demon acting, not her child. This allowed her to remain steadfast in her love for her child despite her child treating her coldly and cutting her out of important events in her life— including her wedding.

For other targeted parents, the image is that the child is a puppet being controlled by the alienating parent or that the child is like those nested wooden dolls, with the true child trapped inside the brittle outer layers of the false selves. Another parent called on the image of his child as a shining beautiful newborn, which helped him to recapture the awe in his child's innocence and vulnerability.

Exercise 8.8: Develop an Image

Take the time to consciously and deliberately consider different images and metaphors until you find one that works for you. Consider typing it up or writing it by hand on beautiful paper and posting it around your house so that you are face to face with it several times each day. Find ways to make it your own.

Validate Your Identity as a Parent

Some targeted parents find that they no longer feel or are perceived by others as a true parent once their children have cut them off. Their children have devalued them and these parents can sometimes internalize the negative message that they are not worthy people and are not real or true parents. They have been erased and replaced through the alienation process. One mother wrote that she attended her son's high school graduation: "I saw how tall and handsome Ethan was standing in his cap and gown. When they asked parents of the graduates to stand up, I didn't know what to do." Metaphorically and literally, you must continue to stand up as your child's parent, as this mother did. It is through maintaining your identity as a parent that you will find the strength for your parental alienation journey. It is through knowing that your children are still your children and that they need you, even though they cannot tell you and may not always know it themselves, that you will find the courage to forge ahead. Because of the outward pressure to negate your role as a parent, you will have to consciously affirm your right to the title of *parent* and your right to claim that role as part of your identity.

Like the mantra and the metaphor, you will need to put deliberate effort into finding ways to validate your parenthood. For example, you might find pictures of yourself with your children in a loving embrace and place the picture where you will see it and draw strength from it. You might benefit from doing the same with Mother's Day/Father's Day cards and letters written to you by your pre-alienated children.

Exercise 8.9: Validate Your Identity as a Parent

Consider ways to validate your identity as a parent through photographs, letters, cards, gifts, and loving memories of your time together with your children. Find ways to remind yourself that you are a parent and that your children need you.

CONCLUSION

Living with parental alienation is excruciating and heartbreaking. Targeted parents experience a range of negative emotions over (typically) an extended period of time. The process of being alienated and the efforts to reconnect with the lost child can be all-consuming. We encourage targeted parents to feel their feelings but, in doing so, to be mindful of the impact of these feelings on themselves and to take care of themselves through their alienation journey. We also encourage targeted parents to periodically take a step back to experience themselves as more than just a targeted parent and, thereby, to not let the alienation define them. They need to take care of themselves in order to forge ahead in their alienation journey.

Chapter Nine

Strategies for Reconnecting with Adult Alienated Children

In this final chapter we will offer targeted parents concrete suggestions for sparking a reconciliation with a currently alienated child. To do so, we will draw on the lessons learned from the stories submitted for this book, as well as collective wisdom gained over the years. Needless to say, there is no magic bullet or magic wand that will work for every child.

EXPLORE THE ALIENATION FROM YOUR CHILD'S POINT OF VIEW

You have a story to tell. We have never met a targeted parent who did not want to tell their story, to be heard, to be understood, to be validated. Yours is a story of abuse of power (of the system, of your ex, and, to an extent, of your child). Yours is a story of heartbreak. But your story is not your child's story. In order to help break through the impasse, you need to reorient yourself to think about the alienation from your child's perspective. Specifically, you need to think about what poisonous messages your child received about you and what, in your actions, attitudes, and behavior, inadvertently reinforced that negative message—at least from your child's point of view.

In our experience, certain themes or elements are common across alienation stories, such as which parent moved out of the home (that parent can be made to appear as if he or she were abandoning the child), how money is being spent (one parent can always make it appear as if the other parent is being greedy and selfish), and which parent becomes involved in a new relationship first (that parent can be made to seem as if she or he were moving on and abandoning the child). But the truth is, almost any action or attitude can be cast in a negative light (e.g., a stay-at-home parent can be presented as lazy and entitled, while a working parent can be portrayed as preoccupied and selfish). So the key is thinking about the unfolding alienation drama from your child's point of view.

Your point of view might be that your child was afraid of losing the love of her father, so she cut you off to please him. Or your story might be that your son felt responsible for his emotionally fragile mother and so became angry at you in order to have an excuse for refusing to visit and thereby please his mother. But your child most likely doesn't see it that way—at least not yet. Therefore you must avoid presenting your version of the story to your child, as it will only create distance, if not anger. Nothing can be gained from writing or speaking to your child and saying, "Another year has gone by where your mother hasn't allowed me to see you" or "If your father hadn't taken me to court and wasted all of my money, I would have bought you a gift." You may reap the momentary satisfaction of speaking your mind, but that is all.

We suggest you seek out information so that you can consider the alienation from your child's point of view. Start by asking yourself what messages your child received about you that warped his or her view of you, changing it from one of a loving parent to a parent who was unsafe, unloving, and unavailable. Then think about what you did (even things you did for the right reasons and things that were not objectively bad) that inadvertently supported the negative message about you. It also may help to jog your memory or create the proper frame of mind to ponder what your child would say to a friend about why he or she no longer has contact with you. It is highly unlikely that your child would say, "Well, when I was about ten years old my parents got divorced and my mother manipulated me into thinking my father was a bad guy when he really wasn't, and so I haven't spoken to him since then." Most likely, if your child had been aware of the manipulation that resulted in the alienation, you would have a relationship with him or her. Thus, your child probably has some explanation for the breach that does not involve being manipulated into alienation, and that explanation, no matter how false or reductive, is what you want to tap into. Once you understand the alienation from your child's point of view, you have a common language for exploring and discussing his experiences. Once you feel that you have at least the beginning of an understanding, you can approach your child through a letter.

WRITE A LETTER TO YOUR CHILD

Once you think you have a handle on your child's perspective, we encourage you to write a letter to your child. This will probably be different from other letters, as it will have a number of important elements.

Opening

Begin the letter with a brief heartfelt opening, such as "My darling daughter" or "Dearest Son."

Acknowledge the Breach

Next, you want to demonstrate that you have a shared reality about the fact that you don't currently have a warm and close relationship (if any). You can say something like "It has been such a long time since we have been close" or "I have been thinking a lot lately about the distance in our relationship." Do not mention the other parent or parental alienation, or in any way lay the blame for the breach anywhere.

Express a Desire for Improvement

Make your desires known by saying, "I so want a better relationship with you" or "I very much want to heal the breach between us." You can add, "I love you so much and want nothing more than to move beyond the hurt and anger between us." Do not add anything that sounds guilt provoking or pathetic, such as "I weep for my lost child" or "I haven't smiled since the day you left." This would seem self-serving.

Offer a Vision of a Better Future

In order to help your child save face, you want to offer the idea that the breach can be healed. You might say, "Sometimes parents and their adult children become estranged [don't say alienated]; often they can find a way to work things out that feels right for everyone. I very much want that to happen with us." Notice the mutuality of the statement.

Acknowledge the Hurt and Anger

Show empathy for your child's suffering: "I can see (or sense) that you are feeling hurt and angry with me and I am so sorry for the pain that I have caused you." Now is not the time to parse blame or to play it safe by saying ". . . for the pain that I may have caused you" or ". . . for any way in which you feel that I might have hurt you." This will seem obviously insincere (or self-serving) to your child.

Wonder What the Problem Is

Here is where you take a stab at what is bothering your child. You want to offer this with the word "wonder" to show that you are not being intrusive or telling your child what he is feeling. So you might say, "I am wondering if you are hurt and angry when it seemed like I wasn't willing to pay for your private school" or "I am wondering if you are feeling upset about how I said I couldn't buy that horse for you." Make sure to add an ending to this portion by saying, "I would very much like to hear and understand what your feelings are, so I can understand from your point of view what this has been like for you."

Invite Working Things Out

You can now offer to your child various options for him or her to share his or her perspective with you. Make sure that it is clear that you are not offering to debate or enlighten. So you could try something like "I would like to offer you the opportunity to share your perspective with me about what is bothering you. I promise that I will not share my perspective unless you want me to. We could do this in writing, on the phone, in person, or with a therapist of your choosing." (Make sure to say this, or else your child will think you are trying to set up an ambush in your therapist's office.) Close this portion with a hope for reparation, such as "I very much want to understand your feelings so that I can try to make up to you for the ways in which you have been hurt."

Spark a Sense Memory

At this point in the letter you want to spark a memory that involves smell or taste. Here are some examples: "I was walking by the Flakey Bakery the other day and stopped in to smell their fresh bread. Remember how we used to go there and get those big cookies after school on Fridays!" Or "I took a walk in Spring Park the other day when the leaves were turning and the nature path smelled of fresh earth and the air smelled so sweet. We used to take walks there every Saturday morning when you were little. You loved to crunch the leaves under your feet!" Or "I baked Grandma's lasagna the other night and added the fresh mozzarella just the way you liked it. You really enjoyed layering the warm tomato sauce on the steaming noodles. The whole house smelled of cheese! And the recipe was as good as ever."

The memory should be a positive memory of something the two of you did together often enough that your child is likely to recall it, and it should involve a pleasant smell. If you have a photograph of the two of you from that time, that would be helpful as well. The photograph should depict warm and positive emotions shared between the two of you. You can mention that you just came across the photo, put it on your fridge, and made a copy for your child.

End the Letter

The letter should end as it began—with an expression of love and caring for your child and a desire for a reparation of the breach. You also want to reassure your child that your heart is open, your arms are open, and your door is open. You could say, "Please know that you can reach me any time at [insert your number if your child doesn't have it]. I want nothing more than to move forward in our relationship."

Review the Letter

Have a close friend read the letter and make sure that it is not too maudlin, weak, angry, or anything else that you want to avoid. Don't send it right away. Let it sit or marinate for a day or two to see, as you go about your daily life, what else comes to mind that you might want to include in the letter.

Send the Letter

As long as you have a way to get the letter to your child, you should send it.

Keep Your Expectations Low

While it would be great if the letter provoked an immediate positive response, that is not going to happen each and every time (although it has happened in some cases). There are three likely responses. First, your child could respond in a positive manner, agreeing to share thoughts and feelings with you. Second, your child could respond with anger. And third, your child could not respond at all. It might be helpful to think of each of these as a good outcome.

If your child offers to share his or her perspective with you, then you will have a clear opportunity to heal the breach and hopefully move forward. If your child responds with anger, you can also think of that as a good thing in that any response is a good sign. Even if your child sends you a nasty letter in response, it is still the beginning of a dialogue. You can respond with empathy and love and an effort to understand what your child is telling you. And should your child not respond at all, you can gain some solace from knowing that you are doing everything you can to bridge the divide, including writing a letter that may provoke some question or doubt in your child's mind about who you are and what you mean to him.

FOLLOW UP WITH FREQUENT MESSAGES OF LOVE AND CONNECTION

You probably need to be reaching out to your child about once a week with a brief text message or e-mail (assuming you have access), to send your child a message of love. Avoid guilt-provoking or self-pitying messages and obviously do not mention the other parent, discuss your version of events, or mention the concept of parental alienation.

In order to avoid despair, it may help to think of your messages of love as watering a plant. When we plant a seed in the ground, we cannot see what is happening beneath the earth, but we water the soil anyway. The watering is an act of hope and faith that one day a flower will bloom. Your relationship with your child is like that flower. It needs attention and care every day so that one day—perhaps when you least expect it—that flower will bloom and your child will respond to you with the openness of love.

Final Words

We began this project by inviting targeted parents to take a journey with us by sharing their stories of parental alienation. We believed and hoped that in doing so there would be something valuable for both the reader and the storyteller. Through the telling and reading of stories about parental alienation—despite the grief and despair so prevalent throughout those stories—we can get closer to the truth of our own experiences and come to better understand the truths of others. And knowing and honoring this truth—as painful as that truth is—can bring its own kind of healing and refuge; as said by Tara Brach, "Presence is the essence of true refuge."[1]

Since we began this project, we have been so impressed with the diligence and courage of the parents who strove to tell their stories and those who actually made submissions for the book. Most found the invitation compelling, but also challenging. We received many e-mails from parents describing the difficulty they were experiencing in putting their pain into words, choosing which of the many excruciating moments to highlight and which to let remain in the dark. For some, the task was too painful, while for others it seemed to offer relief. We appreciate the heroic effort that all of the parents put into this project, regardless of whether their story was submitted or whether it was included in the book. Each story is a gem.

Each story tells the tale of a child torn between two parents and the story of a parent who, despite loving his or her child, loses that child at least for a while. We try to make sense of these stories so that others can better understand the phenomenon of parental alienation, so that perhaps fewer people will have to go through it in the future, and so that those who do will feel less alone. As Judy Collins wrote after the death of her son, "We have to tell our own story, and find our own peace and our own light on this path of loss."[2]

We want to close this book with our sincerest appreciation for both storytellers and readers. You are not alone.

Notes

1. INTRODUCTION

1. Lyric excerpt from the Broadway musical *Once on This Island*. Lyrics by Lynn Ahrens. Lyrics copyright 1991, Hillsdale Music, Inc.

2. R. J. Riordan, F. Mullis, & L. Nuchow (1996), Organizing for bibliotherapy: The science of the art, *Individual Psychology, 52*(2), 169–180.

3. A. J. L. Baker (2006), The power of stories/Stories about power: Why therapists and clients should read stories about the parental alienation syndrome, *American Journal of Family Therapy, 34*(3), 191–203.

4. D. T. Taylor (1996), *The healing power of stories* (New York: Doubleday), p. 6.

5. D. Rooks (2001), *Spinning gold out of straw: How stories heal* (St. Augustine, FL: Salt Run Press), p. 210.

6. American Psychiatric Association (2013), *Diagnostic and statistical manual*, 5th edition (Washington, DC: Author), p. 810.

7. J. Johnston (2003), Parental alignments and rejection: An empirical study of alienation in children of divorce, *Journal of the American Academy of Psychiatry and the Law, 31*(2), 158–170.

8. A. J. L. Baker (2007), *Adult children of parental alienation syndrome: Breaking the ties that bind* (New York: W. W. Norton).

9. A. J. L. Baker & D. Darnall (2006), Behaviors and strategies of parental alienation: A survey of parental experiences, *Journal of Divorce and Remarriage, 45*(1/2), 97–124.

10. A. J. L. Baker (2010), Adult recall of parental alienation in a community sample: Prevalence and associations with psychological maltreatment, *Journal of Divorce and Remarriage, 51*(1), 16–35; A. J. L. Baker & M. R. Brassard (in press), Adolescents caught in their parents' loyalty conflicts, *Journal of Divorce and Remarriage, 54*(5), 393–413; A. J. L. Baker & A. Eichler (in press), College student childhood exposure to parental loyalty conflicts, *Families in Society*; A. J. L. Baker & M. C. Verrocchio (in press), Italian college student childhood exposure to parental loyalty conflicts, *Journal of Divorce and Remarriage*; A. J. L. Baker & N. Ben Ami (2011), To turn a child against a parent is to turn a child against himself, *Journal of Divorce and Remarriage, 54*(2), 203–219.

11. R. Gardner (1998), *Parental alienation: A guide for mental health and legal professionals* (Cresskill, NJ: Creative Therapeutics, Inc.).

12. A. J. L. Baker & D. Darnall (2007), A construct study of the eight symptoms of severe parental alienation syndrome: A survey of parental experiences, *Journal of Divorce and Remarriage, 47*(1), 55–75.

13. A. J. L. Baker, B. Burkhard, & J. Kelly (2012), Differentiating alienated from not alienated children: A pilot study, *Journal of Divorce and Remarriage, 53*(3), 178–193.

14. J. B. Kelly & J. R. Johnston (2001), A reformulation of parental alienation syndrome, *Family Court Review, 39*(3), 249–266.

15. See J. Briere (1992), *Child abuse trauma: Theory and treatment of the lasting effects* (Thousand Oaks, CA: Sage).

16. M. Freeman (2009), *Hindsight: The promise and peril of looking back* (Oxford: Oxford University Press), p. 7.

3. IF I KNEW THEN WHAT I KNOW NOW

1. R. J. Stenack (2001), *Stop controlling me! What to do when someone you love has too much power over you* (Oakland, CA: New Harbinger), p. 5.

2. Ibid.

3. Ibid., p. 9.

4. B. Marshall (2007), *Deal breakers: When to work on a relationship and when to walk away* (New York, NY: Simon Spotlight Entertainment), p. 5.

5. H. Lerner (2002), *The dance of connection* (New York, NY: William Morrow), p. 90.

6. B. DeAngelis (1992), *Are you the one for me? Knowing who's right and avoiding who's wrong* (New York, NY: Delacorte Press), p. 8.

7. Ibid.

8. Marshall (2007), *Deal breakers*, p. 10.

9. Ibid.

10. C. Tavris & E. Aronson (2007), *Mistakes were made (but not by me)* (New York, NY: Harcourt), p. 95.

11. G. Simon (1996), *In sheep's clothing: Understanding and dealing with manipulative people*, revised edition (Little Rock, AK: Patkhurst Brothers).

12. L. Bancroft (2002), *Why does he do that? Inside the minds of angry and controlling men* (New York, NY: Putnam Books).

13. J. Gottman (1994), *Why marriages succeed or fail* (New York, NY: Simon & Schuster).

14. M. Gladwell (2007), *Blink* (New York, NY: Little, Brown).

15. Bancroft (2002), *Why does he do that?*.

16. American Psychiatric Association (2013), *Diagnostic and statistical manual* (Washington, DC: Author), p. 669.

5. THE ALIENATION TIPPING POINT

1. M. Gladwell (2002), *The tipping point* (New York, NY: Little, Brown).

2. J. Lehrer (2009), *How we decide* (New York, NY: Houghton Mifflin), p. 211.

3. D. DiSalvo (2011), *What makes your brain happy and why you should do the opposite* (New York, NY: Prometheus).

4. C. Tavris & E. Aronson (2007), *Mistakes were made (but not by me)* (New York, NY: Harcourt), p. 2.

5. DiSalvo (2011), *What makes your brain happy.*

6. Gladwell (2002), *The tipping point*, p. 73.

7. W. L. Bremback & W. S. Howell (1976), *Persuasion: A means of social influence*, 2nd edition (Englewood, NJ: Prentice-Hall), p. 251.

8. Gladwell (2002), *The tipping point*, p. 256.

9. Ibid., p. 80.

10. R. V. Levine (2003), *The power of persuasion: How we're bought and sold* (New York, NY: Wiley).

11. P. Brinol & R. E. Petty (2003), Overt head movements and persuasion: A self-validation analysis, *Journal of Personality and Social Psychology, 84*, 1123–1139.

12. R. Cialdini (2006), *Influence: The psychology of persuasion* (New York, NY: Harper-Business).

13. Ibid., p. 57.

14. Ibid., p. 92.

15. Lehrer (2009), *How we decide.*

16. S. Miller (2012), Clinical reasoning and decision making in cases of child alignment: Diagnostic and therapeutic issues, in A. J. L. Baker & S. R. Sauber (Eds.), *Working with alienated children and families: A clinical guidebook* (New York, NY: Routledge), pp. 8–46.

17. J. Johnston (2003), Parental alignments and rejection: An empirical study of alienation in children of divorce, *Journal of the American Academy of Psychiatry and the Law, 31*(2), 158–170, p. 169.

7. HOPE AND HEALING

1. A. J. L. Baker (2007), *Adult children of parental alienation syndrome: Breaking the ties that bind* (New York: W.W. Norton).

2. P. Zimbardo (2007), *The Lucifer effect* (New York, NY: Random House).

3. G. J. Thompson & J. B. Jenkins (1993), *Verbal judo: The gentle art of persuasion* (New York, NY: William Morrow), p. 23.

4. Ibid., p. 67.

5. D. J. Lieberman (2002), *Make peace with anyone: Breakthrough strategies to quickly end any conflict, feud, or estrangement* (New York: St. Martin's).

8. LIVING WITH ALIENATION

1. E. Kübler-Ross (1997), *On death and dying* (New York: Scribner).

2. Chronic Pain Anonymous Service Board (2012), *Stories of hope: Living in serenity with chronic pain and illness* (Scottsdale, AZ: Author), p. 7.

3. K. Lebow (2012), Supporting targeted parents: The International Support Network for Alienated Families, in A. J. L. Baker & S. R. Sauber (Eds.), *Working with alienated children and families: A clinical guidebook* (New York, NY: Routledge), pp. 129–148.

4. W. Goldberg & L. Goldberg (2012), Psychotherapy with targeted parents, in A. J. L. Baker & S. R. Sauber (Eds.), *Working with alienated children and families: A clinical guidebook* (New York, NY: Routledge), pp. 108–128.

FINAL WORDS

1. T. Brach (2013), *True refuge* (New York: Bantam Books), p. 10.

2. J. Collins (2007), *The seven T's: Finding hope and healing in the wake of tragedy* (New York, NY: Jeremy P. Tarcher/Penguin), p. 5.

References

Ahrens, L. (1991). Why we tell the story, from *Once on this island*. Hillsdale Music, Inc.

American Psychiatric Association. (2013). *Diagnostic and statistical manual of mental disorders* (5th ed.). Washington, DC: American Psychiatric Association.

Baker, A. J. L. (2006). The power of stories/Stories about power: Why therapists and clients should read stories about the parental alienation syndrome. *American Journal of Family Therapy, 34*(3), 191–203.

Baker, A. J. L. (2007). *Adult children of parental alienation syndrome: Breaking the ties that bind*. New York: W. W. Norton.

Baker, A. J. L. (2010). Adult recall of parental alienation in a community sample: Prevalence and associations with psychological maltreatment. *Journal of Divorce and Remarriage, 51*(1), 16–35.

Baker, A. J. L., & Ben Ami, N. (2011). To turn a child against a parent is to turn a child against himself. *Journal of Divorce and Remarriage, 54*(2), 203–219.

Baker, A. J. L., & Brassard, M. R. (2013). Adolescents caught in their parents' loyalty conflicts. *Journal of Divorce and Remarriage, 54*(5), 393–413.

Baker, A. J. L., Burkhard, B., & Kelly, J. (2012). Differentiating alienated from not alienated children: A pilot study. *Journal of Divorce and Remarriage, 53*(3), 178–193.

Baker, A. J. L., & Chambers, J. (2011). Adult recall of childhood exposure to parental conflict: Unpacking the black box of parental alienation. *Journal of Divorce and Remarriage, 52*(1), 55–76.

Baker, A. J. L., & Darnall, D. (2006). Behaviors and strategies of parental alienation: A survey of parental experiences. *Journal of Divorce and Remarriage, 45*(1/2), 97–124.

Baker, A. J. L., & Darnall, D. (2007). A construct study of the eight symptoms of severe parental alienation syndrome: A survey of parental experiences. *Journal of Divorce and Remarriage, 47*(1), 55–75.

Baker, A. J. L., & Eichler, A. (in press). College student childhood exposure to parental loyalty conflicts. *Families in Society*.

Baker, A. J. L., & P. Fine. (in press). *Co-parenting with a toxic ex: What to do when your ex-spouse tries to turn the kids against you*. Oakland, CA: New Harbinger.

Baker, A. J. L., & R. Sauber, eds. (2013). *Working with alienated children and families: A clinical guidebook*. New York: Routledge.

167

Baker, A. J. L., & Verrocchio, M. C. (in press). Italian college student childhood exposure to parental loyalty conflicts. *Journal of Divorce and Remarriage*.

Baldwin, A. (2009). *A promise to ourselves*. New York: St. Martin's.

Bancroft, L. (2002). *Why does he do that? Inside the minds of angry and controlling men*. New York: G. P. Putnam's Sons.

Brach, T. (2013). *True refuge*. New York: Bantam Books.

Brembeck, W. L., & Howell, W. S. (1976). *Persuasion: A means of social influence* (2nd ed.). Englewood, NJ: Prentice-Hall.

Briere, J. (1992). *Child abuse trauma: Theory and treatment of the lasting effects*. Thousand Oaks, CA: Sage.

Brinol, P., & Petty, R. E. 2003. Overt head movements and persuasion: A self-validation analysis. *Journal of Personality and Social Psychology, 84*, 1123–1139.

Chronic Pain Anonymous Service Board. 2012. *Stories of hope: Living in serenity with chronic pain and illness*. Scottsdale, AZ: Author.

Cialdini, R. (2006). *Influence: The psychology of persuasion*. New York: HarberBusiness.

Collins, J. (2007). *The seven T's: Finding hope and healing in the wake of tragedy*. New York: Jeremy P. Tarcher/Penguin.

DeAngelis, B. (1992). *Are you the one for me? Knowing who's right and avoiding who's wrong*. New York: Delacorte Press.

DiSalvo, D. (2011). *What makes your brain happy and why you should do the opposite*. Amherst, NY: Prometheus Books.

Freeman, M. (2009). *Hindsight: The promise and peril of looking back*. Oxford: Oxford University Press.

Gardner, R. (1998). *Parental alienation: A guide for mental health and legal professionals*. Cresskill, NJ: Creative Therapeutics, Inc.

Gladwell, M. (2002). *The tipping point*. New York: Little, Brown.

Gladwell, M. (2007). *Blink*. New York: Little, Brown.

Goldberg, W., & Goldberg, L. (2013). Psychotherapy with targeted parents. In A. J. L. Baker & S. R. Sauber (Eds.), *Working with alienated children and families: A clinical guidebook* (pp. 108–128). New York: Routledge.

Gottman, J. (1994). *Why marriages succeed or fail*. New York: Simon & Schuster.

Johnston, J. (2003). Parental alignments and rejection: An empirical study of alienation in children of divorce. *Journal of the American Academy of Psychiatry and the Law, 31*(2), 158–170.

Kelly, J. B., & Johnston, J. R. (2001). A reformulation of parental alienation syndrome. *Family Court Review, 39*(3), 249–266.

Kübler-Ross, E. (1997). *On death and dying*. New York: Scribner.

Lebow, K. (2013). Supporting targeted parents: The International Support Network for Alienated Families. In A. J. L. Baker & S. R. Sauber (Eds.), *Working with alienated children and families: A clinical guidebook* (pp. 129–148). New York: Routledge.

Lehrer, J. (2009). *How we decide*. New York: Houghton Mifflin Harcourt.

Lerner, H. (2002). *The dance of connection*. New York: William Morrow.

Levine, R. V. (2003). *The power of persuasion: How we're bought and sold*. New York: John Wiley & Sons.

Lieberman, D. J. (2002). *Make peace with anyone: Breakthrough strategies to quickly end any conflict, feud, or estrangement*. New York: St. Martin's.

Marshall, B. (2007). *Deal breakers: When to work on a relationship and when to walk away*. New York: Simon Spotlight Entertainment.

Miller, S. G. (2013). Clinical reasoning and decision-making in cases of child-alignment: Diagnostic and therapeutic issues. In A. J. L. Baker & S. R. Sauber (Eds.), *Working with alienated children and families: A clinical guidebook* (pp. 8–46). New York: Routledge.

Riordan, R. J., Mullis, F., & Nuchow, L. (1996). Organizing for bibliotherapy: The science of the art. *Individual Psychology, 52*(2), 169–180.

Rooks, D. (2001). *Spinning gold out of straw: How stories heal.* St. Augustine, FL: Salt Run Press.

Simon, G. (1996). *In sheep's clothing: Understanding and dealing with manipulative people* (Rev. ed.). Little Rock, AK: Parkhurst Brothers.

Stenack, R. J. (2001). *Stop controlling me! What to do when someone you love has too much power over you.* Oakland, CA: New Harbinger Publications.

Tavris, C., & Aronson, E. (2007). *Mistakes were made (but not by me).* New York: Harcourt.

Taylor, D. T. (1996). *The healing power of stories.* New York: Doubleday.

Thompson, G. J., & Jenkins, J. B. (1993). *Verbal judo: The gentle art of persuasion.* New York: William Morrow.

Verrocchio, M. C., & Baker, A. J. L. (in press). Italian adults recall of childhood exposure to parental loyalty conflicts. *Journal of Child and Family Studies.*

Zimbardo, P. (2007). *The Lucifer effect.* New York: Random House.

Index

About the Authors

Amy J. L. Baker is a leading national expert on parental alienation and children caught in loyalty conflicts and is the author of several books on the topic, including *Adult Children of Parental Alienation Syndrome: Breaking the Ties That Bind* (2007), *Working with Alienated Children and Families: A Clinical Guidebook*, which was coedited with Richard Sauber (2013), and *Co-Parenting with a Toxic Ex: What to Do When Your Ex-Spouse Tries to Turn the Kids Against You* (forthcoming), coauthored with Paul Fine. She is a parenting coach and conducts trainings around the country for parents and legal and mental health professionals, has written dozens of scholarly articles on topics related to parent-children relationships, and has appeared on national television. Dr. Baker has a PhD in human development from Teachers College of Columbia University.

Paul R. Fine is a licensed clinical social worker with over twenty-years experience working with children, couples, and families. With Dr. Baker, he is the coauthor of two articles on children caught in loyalty conflicts and the forthcoming book *Co-Parenting with a Toxic Ex.*